Falconry & Hawking

The Essential Handbook

Including Equipment, Training and Health

By Philip Golding

Copyright and Trademarks

Disclaimer and Legal Notice

This product is not legal, accounting, medical or health advice and should not be interpreted in that manner. You need to do your own due-diligence to determine if the content of this product is right for you and your animals. While we have tried to verify the information in this publication, neither the author, publisher nor the affiliates assume any responsibility for errors, omissions or contrary interpretation of the subject matter herein.

We have no control over the nature, content and availability of the web sites, products or sources listed in this book. The inclusion of any web site links does not necessarily imply a recommendation or endorsement of the views expressed within them. We may receive payment if you order a product or service using a link contained within this book. BLEP Publishing or the author take no responsibility or will not be liable for the websites or content being unavailable or removed.

The advice and strategies, contained herein may not be suitable for every individual or animal / pet. The author and publisher shall not be liable for any loss incurred as a consequence of the use and or the application, directly or indirectly, of any information presented in this work. This publication is designed to provide information in regard to the subject matter covered.

Neither the author nor the publisher assume any responsibility for any errors or omissions, nor do they represent or warrant that the information, ideas, plans, actions, suggestions, and methods of operation contained herein is in all cases true, accurate, appropriate, or legal. It is the reader's responsibility to consult with his or her own advisor before putting any of the enclosed information, ideas, or practices written in this book in to practice.

Foreword

For many in the modern world, falconry has become associated purely with the idea of a demonstration event with birds of prey often seen at Renaissance Faires or other medieval re-enactments. The sport itself seems to be almost a quaint anachronism from a long-ago age, more a curiosity than a living and viable art form.

Consequently, it comes as a shock to many that the ancient art of falconry is still being practiced worldwide today, or that falcons continue to be of service to man in our modern, machine-oriented world. Far from being merely props at Renaissance Faires, trained falcons are highly intelligent creatures whose long association with humankind continues to evolve.

For instance, falcons have been used with great success at airports around the world, including New York's JFK to keep the runways clear of nuisance birds. If left unchecked, these creatures, including sea gulls, can cause flight delays and serious accidents if they are sucked into the jet engines or collide with a plane's windshield.

In cities in the American south, routinely plagued by black clouds of grackles migrating to Mexico, falcons are called in to drive the filthy birds away from parking lots and out of heavily infested trees where their excrement creates a huge urban headache.

Around the world, dedicated falconers keep the traditions of the sport alive, flying their birds as the hunters they were born to be. The deep bond that forms between raptor and man is one built on mutual respect, and, is a thing so elemental, it's difficult to describe to those who have not experienced it for themselves.

I cannot stress strongly enough that falconry is at its heart a mentorship sport. In the United States you cannot earn a falconry license unless you work with a master falconer, and this is still the best way to absorb the intricacies of both the sport and of the husbandry of the birds themselves.

In the following pages, I will provide a brief history of falconry and profiles of some of the most popular birds used in the sport. This will be followed by a breakdown of the basic steps to becoming an apprentice falconer, a consideration of the equipment needed to get involved in the sport, and an overview of healthcare and husbandry for captive raptors.

Please understand that 20 years into the sport, you will still be learning about your birds and trying out new techniques for training and flying them. Falconry is a living, breathing art form, and one that is kept alive and vital by engaged practitioners. There are indeed "falcon whisperers" out there, and if you have the chance to work with a master falconer, no matter your own level of experience, don't pass up the chance!

My goal here is to provide you with a comprehensive introduction to the sport. This book may best serve those with an existing interest in falconry who have not yet committed to the lifestyle. Yes, lifestyle. Falconry, although called a sport, is not a hobby, nor is it a pastime. If you choose to become a falconer, your life will change.

Of falconry, the American ornithologist Roger Tory Peterson said, "Man has emerged from the shadows of antiquity with a Peregrine on his wrist. Its dispassionate brown eyes, more than those of any other bird, have been witness to the struggle for civilization, from the squalid tents on the steppes of Asia thousands of years ago to the marble halls of European kings in the 17th century."

By making the decision to become a part of that legacy, you will be committing yourself to spending hours in the company of a magnificent bird of prey, and you will be accepting full responsibility for its welfare and use as a hunting animal. This is an enormously rewarding decision, but one that should not be made lightly.

Table of Contents

Table of Contents

Table of Contents

Table of Contents

Table of Contents

FREE Falconry Videos

Before I go any further I want to share with a fabulous collection of falconry videos

Please just visit

http://www.FalconryGift.com so we can email all the videos 100% free – just as an extra 'thank you' for purchasing this book.

The videos cover everything including

- Introduction
- Getting Started
- Telemetry
- Training
- Hoods
- Lure
- And lots more

Make sure you receive them free at

http://www.FalconryGift.com

Chapter 1 - Falconry in World Culture

There is great debate among historians and falconers about the true origins of the sport, which is defined as, "the taking of wild quarry in its natural state and habitat by means of a trained raptor."

Clarifying Terminology

Before we delve deeper into this discussion, a few terms should be clarified since many are still used by contemporary practitioners.

- A "falconer" is a person who flies a falcon but the term has become broadly employed for anyone who flies a bird of prey.

- An "austringer" flies either a hawk or an eagle.

- In the early English tradition, the word "falcon" referred to a female falcon only.

- The words "hawk" and "hawke" were used for female hawks.

- Male hawks or falcons were called "tiercels" or "tercels."

- The practice of hunting with a trained or "conditioned" bird of prey is called "hawking" or "gamehawking," but again this is a word often used interchangeably with falconry

(Please see Chapter 7 for a more extensive compilation of falconry terms.)

Origins in Mongolia and the Middle East

Three thousand years ago on the steppes of Mongolia falconers in the army of the Great Khans flew their birds to hunt for food and as a sport to relieve the tedium of campaign life in between battles.

Some historians believe the practice is far older, however, with its true origins lying in Arabia or perhaps in Iran where kings living as long as 10,000 years ago tamed and used birds of prey for hunting. Many experts points to the idea of "parallel evolution" for the training and use of these magnificent birds across multiple cultures.

It was this understanding that led the United Nations Educational Scientific and Cultural Organization (UNESCO) to add falconry to its list of Intangible Cultural Heritages of Humanity on November 16, 2010.

There is ample evidence to support the ancient nature and wide dispersal of falconry. The first complete book on the subject was commissioned in the 12th century by the Persian king Naseraddin Shah, a ruler of the Qajar dynasty. The *Baznameh-e-Naseri* was considered to be so comprehensive and famous, it was translated into English, French and German.

The entire region of the Arabian Gulf was influential in the spread of falconry throughout the Islamic World. There are specific verses in the Holy Koran permitting falconry as a means of hunting. Even today, there is a thriving culture of falconry in the Middle East where working with the birds is believed to teach philosophical lessons in patience, endurance, bravery, and self-reliance.

Falconry in the Asian World

In China, falconry was an integral part of the complex relationship between power and politics as early as 700 BC. The techniques used with falcons, eagles, and other birds of prey are identical to those practiced today and thankfully were preserved for future generations.

Imperial patronage heavily influenced the culture of falconry, which was popular among both the Chinese aristocracy and the common people. However, with the fall of the imperial family in 1912 and the constant period of warfare in the region extending through World War II, falconry all but disappeared from Chinese culture not to be revived until late in the 20th century.

Advances in the Japanese use of birds of prey was delayed by the relative isolation of the home islands. The earliest written accounts of falconry there date from 355 AD and relate to hawks imported from Korea. Falconers worked from horseback armed with bows and were symbolic of military power and dominance. The Japanese tradition is rich with elaborate costumes and equipment, which to this day are aesthetically distinct and very beautiful.

Through the Second World War there were Imperial Falconers, but after the war the art was distributed to the general public through a system of apprenticeships, generally taught by retired imperial falconers.

Falconry in Europe

After becoming well established in the Middle East and Asia by 2,000 BC, falconry gradually spread westward, first entering Italy and Greece and then the remainder of Europe where it surged in popularity from the 6th century forward.

Owning falcons and other birds of prey conveyed status and was considered the purview of royalty and aristocrats. In England, this evolved into a highly stratified code of conduct with various social ranks according the right under the Laws of Ownership to fly specific types of bird.

- gyrfalcons were reserved for kings
- rock falcons for dukes
- peregrines for earls
- goshawks for yeomen
- kestrels for servants

During the reign of Edward III (1237-77) a thief who made off with a trained raptor could be executed for his crime.

One of the most famous of all European Falconers, Frederick II of Hohenstaufen, Holy Roman Emperor, King of Sicily and King of Jerusalem, spent 30 years writing his comprehensive magnum opus on the sport, *The Art of Hunting with Birds or The Art of Falconry* completed in 1274, but not published until 1596. Frederick II was so dedicated to flying birds, he once lost a military campaign because he went hawking rather than attend to the siege of a key fortress.

Falconry diminished alongside the aristocracy in Europe in the 19th century as firearms gained ascendency in the world of hunting for both food and sport. Forest lands were cleared for agriculture, and the ancient art of falconry was actively preserved by only a small population of dedicated enthusiasts.

Falconry in America

Falconry existed in the New World as early as 1500 when the Spanish Conquistadors made note of the Aztec use of trained hawks. The first record of such use among European settlers is found in New England in 1622, but real serious interest began to develop only at the beginning of the 20th century.

The Peregrine Club, the first large falconry association in the United States, was formed in the 1930s, but the sport received scant legal attention until the 1950s.

Falconers themselves proactively sought legal recognition and regulation of their sport with many early advocates involved in ornithology and wildlife management at the professional level.

The North American Falconers Association (NAFA) was founded in 1961 and remains today the backbone of the sport in the U.S. The Association was instrumental in supporting federal jurisdiction over the protection of raptors in the Migratory Bird Treaty in 1972.

In fact, the U.S. Fish & Wildlife Service used specific proposals from NAFA to craft federal falconry regulations. (These laws were just reviewed and revised in 2014.)

Falconry Worldwide

Falconry is still practiced around the world today, with some notable exceptions. The practice is banned in Australia. All native raptors in Australia are protected by the government and none can be owned privately. This is also true in Scandinavia.

Although legal matters will be discussed later in this text, falconry is permitted in the United Kingdom without a license, but only captive-bred birds may be flown. The sport received legal recognition in 1981 as part of the Wildlife and Countryside Act.

Globally it is estimated that about 10,000 individuals legally practice the sport of falconry. Of those more than 5,000 are resident in North America.

Famous Falconers

The pages of history and literature are littered with images and references to famous falconers. It is almost impossible to find a monarch who didn't fly birds of prey, including, but not limited to:

- Charlemagne
- Alexander the Great
- King Richard (The Lionheart)
- Mary, Queen of Scots
- Henry VIII
- Queen Elizabeth I
- Empress Catherine of Russia

The explorer Marco Polo (1254-1324) wrote of Kublai Khan, the grandson of Genghis Khan, "[he] takes with him full 10,000 falconers and some 500 gerfalcons, besides peregrines, sakers, and other hawks in great numbers, and goshawks able to fly at the water-fowl . . ."

The Bayeux tapestry depicting the Norman Conquest of Britain in 1066 shows King Harold of England and William of Normandy hawking together.

Today it is most common to see exhibitions of birds of prey at Medieval and Renaissance Faires. The sport has far from disappeared in our modern world, however, and continues to fascinate would-be falconers.

Be assured, however, that flying a bird of prey is a blood sport, and not an activity for just anyone. The best way to learn to fly a bird is in apprenticeship to a master falconer, an arrangement required by law in the United States to gain your license.

The remainder of this text will explore the types of birds used in "hawking," the required equipment, and the manner in which the birds are trained, as well as provide an overview of captive raptor healthcare and husbandry.

Chapter 2 – Birds Used in Falconry

In general usage, the term "falconry" encompasses the use of several different types of birds of prey for hunting purposes. Some are "beginner's birds" and others should only be kept by those highly experienced in this ancient sport.

As you begin to learn more about the world of falconry, you will become increasingly conversant in the different types of birds you are likely to encounter. The following profiles should serve as a working primer in that regard.

A Note on Acquiring Birds

Before I begin to profile various birds of prey, let me address the most common beginner's concern, "Where do I get my bird?" The answer relies at least in part on the answer to the question, "Where are you?"

In some states in the U.S., for instance, the law requires prospective falconers to trap their own bird. In other cases, you can buy your bird from a breeder. I will address this issue more fully later in this book.

Buzzards

In Great Britain there are three types of buzzards used by falconers. The Common Buzzard is native to the British Isles while the Red-tailed Buzzard and the Ferruginous Buzzard are imports from America where both are referred to as hawks. Both are broad-winged buteos with muscular, sturdy builds.

Buzzards or hawks are regarded as outstanding birds for beginners because they are robust and of a good size. The Red-tailed Buzzard or Hawk, for instance, weighs on average 1.52-3.53 lbs. / 690-1600 grams and has a wingspan of 43-57 inches / 110-145 cm. Females are the larger birds, typically 25% heavier than males.

While smaller birds like the American Kestrel, which is the smallest falcon in North America, might be less frightening to a beginner, they are also tiny and easily harmed at just 7-8 inches in length (19-21 cm) and thus considered useless for falconry by many critics.

Most experts agree that starting with a bird the size of a buzzard or hawk also tests the mettle of the would-be falconer. If the beginner can face and work with an untrained buzzard, enduring bites and footing, they will likely stick it out and become proficient in the end.

(Footing is a term in the sport that refers to a bird attacking the falconer's ungloved hand with its foot. The action is generally deliberate and aggressive.)

Arguably, buzzards are somewhat harder to train initially because, like eagles, they are opportunistic in their approach to feeding themselves. In the wild, these birds will opt for easy, small quarry and even carrion, only going to the effort of taking larger prey when they need to feed their young.

For this reason, master falconers describe them as difficult to "enter," meaning it's hard to introduce the birds to a particular type of quarry. It requires perseverance on the part of the beginning falconer, which not only hones the bird's skills but that of the young apprentice.

It may take 2.5 years to fully train a buzzard, but in that time you can be assured that the apprentice falconer will learn all the necessary lessons in flying and keeping a bird in peak condition. If you begin with a hawk, you can be assured that as you get better at your sport, so will the bird, laying the foundation for a long-term relationship that can last as long as 20 years.

Common Buzzard

In some circles the Common Buzzard (*Buteo buteo*) is somewhat maligned, but in truth the bird's good and steady temperament makes it an excellent beginner's bird.

Also, because they do not travel great distances in flight, they are not easy to lose.

During early training Common Buzzards will bite and foot, requiring caution in handling. With patience, however, the bird can become adept at taking prey including rabbits, squirrels, and even hare and pheasant.

The Common Buzzard can be anywhere from 16-23 inches / 40-58 cm long, with a 43-54 inch / 109-136 cm wingspan. Adults will weigh 0.9-3 lbs. / 427-1364 grams. The species' range covers most of Europe and into Asia.

Plumage varies by region from white to black, but typically displays as shades of brown with a "necklace" of pale feathers.

Red-Tailed Buzzard

The Red-Tailed Buzzard or Hawk *(Buteo jamaicensis)* is very popular in falconry. It does not exist in the wild in Europe, but is used as a sporting bird around the world. When well trained, it will hunt almost anything from small rodents to rabbits.

Although widely used by apprentices, this bird is not easy to train, having a tendency to be both stubborn and lazy if it is not handled correctly. However, when properly trained, they are superb hunting companions.

The Red-Tailed Buzzard measures 18-26 inches / 45-65 cm long, with a 43-57 inch / 110-145 cm wingspan. Adults weigh 1.52-3.53 lbs. / 690-1664 grams. The species ranges from Alaska and Canada throughout North America and south to Panama and the West Indies.

Plumage varies by region and subspecies, but overall this is a blocky bird with a broad shape. The underbelly is whitish with a dark band of brown across the belly. The tail is brick red above and buff-orange below. The cere, (the featherless area above the beak), legs, and feet are all yellow. Young birds have yellow irises that darken to reddish-brown as they age.

Ferruginous Buzzard

The Ferruginous Buzzard is a broad-winged bird common to the open plains of the United States and Canada. They do not function well in closed country, but are ideal for open land and rolling hills.

Although the species requires great patience in training, there is little that the larger females cannot bring down when hunting. The males are too small to take hares, however, and may even be frightened when first presented with a rabbit for quarry.

The Ferruginous Buzzard or Hawk ranges in length from 20 to 27 inches (51-69 cm) and has a wingspan of 48 to 60 inches (122-152 cm). Weight varies greatly by region from 2.3 lbs. / 1050 grams to 3.9 lbs. / 1776 grams.

Adults may be either light or dark morph. The light birds have rusty brown upper parts and are pale on the head, neck, and underparts. There will be rust on both the legs and underwing, with the upper wins being gray. The dark morphs are a deep brown on the upper and under parts, with light areas on the upper and lower wings.

Harris Hawk

The Harris Hawk (*Parabuteo unicinctus*) is widely regarded as a beginner's bird in both the U.S. and Europe. It boasts both extreme intelligence and superior abilities that steadily improve with age and experience. They tame and handle well, requiring little "manning" time. The species displays a playful streak, but can be stubborn by turns.

Typically, Harris Hawks hunt best when they are a little hungry. These powerful birds will fly in cooperative groups and pairs, both in the wild and when trained, a fact that can help a breeding pair to build their bond.

As with most birds of prey, the males are smaller. On average a Harris Hawk will range in length from 18-23 inches / 46-59 cm and have a wingspan of 41-47 inches / 103-120 cm.

Females are typically 35% larger than males, with an average adult weighing 1.2 to 3.6 lbs. / 546-1633 grams.

Their plumage is dark brown changing to a reddish chestnut on the shoulders, thighs, and lining of the wings. There are white markings on the base and tip of the tail, with the legs and cere (upper beak) both being yellow.

Hawks

Hawks are regarded as "sprinters" among the birds of prey and can be easily "entered" onto or "introduced" to quarry in the company of a falconer.

These birds live for the chase, but are high strung and must be acclimated to potential distractions in the environment like farm equipment, dogs, people, and motor vehicles.

True hawks (accipiters) are not birds for beginners, nor are they right for people who do not have time to devote to their training.

Typically the birds that fall into this category are the Goshawk, Sparrowhawk, Cooper's Hawk, and Black Sparrowhawk.

Northern Goshawk

Due to its scarcity, the Northern Goshawk (*Accipiter gentilis*), is very expensive to acquire. The greatest challenge of flying this species is the ease with which it can be lost, to the point that falconers who use the birds often ensure them against this very peril.

A goshawk is a veritable machine with only two speeds – full out and absolutely still – and when he does fall still, it's generally at the top of the most inaccessible tree in the area.

Goshawks are extremely temperamental and must be manned daily to remain tame. They are definitely a species that requires a huge time commitment.

Although exciting to fly, and capable of bringing down almost any prey, this is not a bird for the faint of heart or the "weekend" falconer.

The species is widespread throughout the northern hemisphere and for this reason is typically called simply "Goshawk."

The birds are blue-grey on top and white or gray barred below. In parts of Asia, however, the birds may be completely black or white on top. Adults have a white eye stripe.

Juveniles are brown above over a barred brown lower section. Their eyes are pale yellow, darkening to red or orange by the second year of life.

Males are 10-25% smaller than females. The average size range across both genders is 18-27 inches / 46-69 cm with a wingspan of 35 to 50 inches / 89-127 cm. The weight varies from 1.72 lbs. to 4.85 lbs. / 780-2200 grams.

Sparrowhawks

Of the many types of sparrowhawks found globally, the Black Sparrowhawk (*Accipiter melanoleucus*), a native of Africa, is the largest, measuring 16-21 inches / 40-54 cm with a wingspan of 30-41 inches / 77-105 cm and weighing 1.65-2.16 lbs. / 750-980 grams.

Juveniles are brown and russet with dark streaks on the head and chest with white or light spots on the wings.

Adults have predominantly black plumage with white on the throat and chest. The cross-barred tails have 3-4 pale stripes with 4-5 on the underside of the wings.

They are finely built and best suited for taking other birds mid-air. Sparrowhawks are even more difficult to handle than Goshawks and their talons are susceptible to injury.

The Eurasian Sparrowhawk (*Accipiter nisus*), which is found in northern Europe and Asia, has a more temperamental nature than the Goshawk.

They are small and difficult to train, to the point that males should not be flown by any but the most expert falconers. The slightest drop in weight for this type of Sparrowhawk can lead to severe illness or even death during the colder months.

Adult Eurasian Sparrowhawks measure 11-16 inches / 29-41 cm with a wingspan of 23-31 inches / 59-80 cm and a weight of 3.9-12.1 ounces / 110-342 grams.

Males are slate gray on the upper parts with red-barred under parts. Females are dark brown to greyish brown on top and brown-barred beneath.

If handled as babies as young as two weeks, Sparrowhawks will imprint with their human and be much tamer and easier to fly. This requires daily manning, however, or the bird will revert to its wild demeanor.

The birds can be flown in a very limited amount of space, but they are absolutely not a beginner's species.

Cooper's Hawk

The Cooper's Hawk (*Accipiter cooperii*) is popular with falconers in America who use them to hunt quail. The birds are small, measuring just 14-20 inches / 35-50 cm, with wingspans of 24-37 inches / 62-94 cm, and a weight of 7.8-25 ounces / 220-700 grams.

The birds have short, round wings. Adults have a black cap, red eyes, blue-gray upper parts, and white underparts thinly barred in red. The tail is blue-gray on top with black bars and pale underneath. In juveniles the cap is brown over yellow eyes, with brown upper parts and pale under parts streaked with fine black lines.

The species has a largely undeserved reputation for bad behavior that, when present, is indicative of poor handling. When well trained, the Cooper's Hawk is easy-going and intelligent with few signs of aggressive behavior.

Falcons

Falcons must be flown in open countryside where there are no woods or areas of scrub brush. If the quarry makes it into an area of cover, the falcon will give up the chase. Some enthusiasts, lacking access to the correct landscape, choose to fly falcons to the lure as a pleasure sport.

If you opt for this avenue, understand that in order to keep your falcon appropriately conditioned and tamed, you will be flying the same bird every day in the same way for 15 to 20 years.

Some falconers fly their birds in front of audiences at exhibitions, which can provide more stimuli, but this is a serious consideration. A magnificent bird should not become the victim of your boredom.

Lanner

The Lanner, (*Falco biarmicus*), a medium-sized bird indigenous to Africa, southeast Europe, and the fringes of Asia, has a length of 13.8-19.7 inches / 35-50 cm.

The wingspan falls in a range of 37.8-41.3 inches / 96-105 cm, with the weight at 17.64-31.74 ounces / 500-900 grams depending on gender. As with most birds of prey, the females are larger.

The upper part of the body is grey-brown to slate with a creamy white throat and underparts, often with dark striping or spots.

The head has a characteristic reddish brown crown and distinctive dark eye stripes complete with a downward turning "moustache." The ring around the dark eye is bright yellow. (Note that these colorations will vary by region.)

Shorter, more compact Lanners, with a shape reminiscent of a Peregrine, fly with fast wing beats and make thrilling stoops (head first dives from great heights.) Those that have a lighter build and longer wings and tails tend to soar or float, saving their energy.

This second variation is wonderfully buoyant and exhibits great maneuverability. They are capable of the same kind of heart-stopping stoops, but they tend to wait until they are directly over their quarry before dropping vertically.

Temperamentally, Lanners are lovely birds and falconers who have flown them routinely describe the experience as positive and a real pleasure.

Prairie Falcon

The Prairie Falcon (*Falco mexicanus*) is indigenous to the North American west and is roughly the size of a crow, with an average length of 16 inches / 40 cm, a wingspan of 40 inches / 1 meter, and a weight of 1.6 lbs. / 720 grams. Females can weigh as much as 3.5 lbs. / 1588 grams.

The Prairie Falcon is a courageous bird of prey and an excellent alternative to a Peregrine, but has been underrated in many parts of the world for being temperamental and even aggressive, which is true if the young birds develop any imprinting on humans.

They are rather greedy and persistent, and thus will handle more enclosed country than other falcon types. Although they range far, Prairie Falcons are obedient, but they are not the correct bird for a nervous handler or an inexperienced one. They take steady nerves and plenty of time.

Saker

The Saker, (*Falco cherrug*) is indigenous to Eastern Europe and ranges across Asia and into Manchuria. In the wild, this is a migratory species, wintering in Ethiopia, on the Arabian Peninsula, in northern Pakistan, and in western China.

This migratory nature can be problematic. When Sakers are imported into other parts of the world, they have been known to simply take off on migration when flown, never so much as looking back at their handlers.

They are big birds, measuring 18-22 inches / 47-55 cm in length with a wingspan of 42-50 inches / 105-129 cm. Males weigh 1.6-2 lbs. / 730-900 grams, with the larger females at 2.14-3 lbs. / 970-1300 grams.

Sakers display widely varied colorations, ranging from a uniform chocolate brown to pale sand marked with brown streaks or bars. Some individuals are almost pure white and are especially prized in the Arabic falconry tradition.

Sakers exhibit tremendous versatility, but with some preference for ground game. Because they are greedy by nature, they train well, but patience must be shown in getting them to take a lure in mid-air. Once they get the hang of it, however, there's no further problem.

Due to their size, female Sakers can be clumsy in the beginning, but over time prove to be highly efficient and fit. Males are somewhat more agile, due to their smaller size

Peregrine Falcon

The Peregrine Falcon (*Falco peregrinus peregrinus*) is a large, blue-gray bird of prey with barred white underparts and a black head. Regarded as the fighter jet of the falconry world, a Peregrine can achieve spectacular stoops of 200 mph / 322 km/h. The highest measured speed for a Peregrine was 242 mph / 389 km/h/

Although fast, their shorter wings and tails make them less maneuverable than other falcons, but they do have a good temperament and take well to training. A Peregrine's true domain, however, is open country. If flown in areas with cover, a telemetry transmitter / receiver set-up is a must.

Peregrine Falcons can be found worldwide in all but the extreme arctic regions. The only landmass they do not call home is New Zealand.

The birds are 13-23 inches / 34-58 centimeters in length with a wingspan of 29-47 inches / 74-120 cm. Males weigh 0.73-2.20 lbs. / 330-1000 grams, while females are approximately 30% larger at 1.13-3.30 lbs. / 513-1500 grams.

Gyrfalcon

The Gyrfalcon, (*Falco rusticolus*) is the largest of the falcons. Some females weigh 4.6 lbs. / 2100 grams! The species is widely dispersed throughout the Northern Hemisphere. Consequently, the plumage varies from all white to dark brown by location.

The birds have been highly prized in falconry for centuries, dating back to the time of the Vikings. Their association with man is, therefore, at least 1,500 years old. Gyrfalcons are seen less in the modern sport, however, due to the problems they pose with recovery.

Because Gyrfalcons are indigenous to open, desolate tundras, they are flown to their greatest advantage in similar spaces. They often travel great distances, making telemetry essential for recovery.

As added complications, the species is very expensive, and many birds taken from the wild die quickly in captivity.

Due to the remoteness of their native range, Gyrfalcons are

not exposed to a wide variety of potential avian diseases, and therefore their immune systems have not developed adequate resistance to many illnesses, including avian flu.

While not as maneuverable or flexible as the Peregrine Falcon, Gryfalcons have greater endurance and can achieve horizontal flight speeds of 80.7 mph / 130 km/h. They are impressive and efficient hunters in the correct circumstances.

Males range in length from 19-24 inches / 48-61 cm, with females measuring 20-26 inches / 51-65 cm. The wingspan by genders is 43-51 inches / 110-130 cm and 49-64 inches/124-160 cm respectively. Males weigh 1.8-3 lbs. / 805-1250 grams and females are 2.6-4.6 lbs. / 1180-2100 grams.

Merlin

The Merlin (*Falco columbarius*) is a small bird of prey indigenous to many parts of the Northern Hemisphere. The birds were once called Pigeon Hawks in North America.

They are blue-grey on the back, lightening to silver grey in some subspecies. The buff to orange underparts may be streaked to varying degrees in black or reddish brown.

Although small, Merlins are heavily built and robust. Adult males may weigh no more than 4.4 to 7.4 ounces / 125-210 grams while the larger females are 6.7 to 10.6 ounces / 190 to 300 grams. The birds range in length from 9.4 to 13 inches / 24-33 cm and have a wingspan of 20-29 inches / 50-73 cm.

Merlins have an excellent reputation for taking quickly to training, but their small size makes them unsuited as a beginner's bird. They are also difficult birds to keep, being prone to developing the parasitic disease coccidiosis, which causes severe diarrhea.

Although the birds normally survive a bout of the disease, they will continue to experience flare ups for life when subjected to stress.

Kestrel

The Kestrel is indigenous to North America, with 15 or more subspecies found in a range that extends to the tip of South America. In fact, the species now enjoys almost global distribution, but it is not a traditional bird in the European or Middle Eastern falconry traditions.

In Great Britain, experts describe the kestrel as a nice aviary bird, but disparage it as an option for a beginner's bird or even one that advanced falconers would find of interest.

Perhaps the best way to describe this species is that it holds its own niche in the falconry world, one that rests purely on American origins.

The Kestrel, (*Falco tinnunculus*) is a small bird, with some rather remarkable abilities. By positioning themselves toward even the slightest headwind, they can hover, even indoors.

For this reason, the Common Kestrel is sometimes referred to as the "Windhover." Although there are different types of Kestrels, the American Kestrel is used widely by falconers in the U.S. and is greatly beloved by those who fly the birds.

Males have white underparts with black barring, a rufous back barred on the lower half, and blue-grey wings. The belly and flanks are white with black spots. Females are cream or buff on the underside with brown streaking, and rufous tails marked by numerous black bars.

The American Kestrel is only 7-8 inches / 19-21 cm long, with some females reaching a length of 10.6 inches / 27 cm. Males weigh 2.8-3.7 ounces / 80-105 grams, while females are 3.5-4.2 ounces / 100-120 grams.

Clearly a bird this small isn't going to take down large prey, but will go after mice, smaller birds, and insects. In the American falconry tradition, Kestrels are less intimidating for beginners, and allow enthusiasts with limited access to land to still enjoy the sport.

Eagles

The use of eagles in falconry demands access to open countryside in unpopulated areas. These large birds are quite capable of killing small dogs. Only the most experienced and responsible falconers should even consider flying eagles.

Because they are highly individualist eagles that often do not take well to being handled by more than one person. Due to their size, basic training practices must be altered to accommodate their bulk.

For instance, rather than being trained to come to the fist, most people opt to call the eagle to a perch or on the ground.

Although intelligent, eagles tend to be lazy. They require a long period of time to relax and become tamed and are somewhat notorious for displays of temper. This is definitely not a class of raptor to be taken up lightly.

There are certainly falconers that have tried working with other eagle species and accounts of their efforts can be found online, but the two seen most often in the sport are the Golden Eagle and the Tawny Eagle.

Golden Eagle

The Golden Eagle (*Aquila chrysaetos*), is widely distributed throughout the Northern Hemisphere. Overall the bird is dark brown, with lighter, golden plumage on the nape (the area from the base of the skull to the upper back.) Immature specimens show white on the tail and wings.

The average length for a Golden Eagle is 26-40 inches (66-

102 cm) with a wingspan of 5 feet 11 inches to 7 feet 9 inches (1.8-2.34 meters).

Females can weigh as much as 14 lbs. (6.35 kg). Depending on the subspecies, some males may weigh as little as 5.5 lbs. (2.5 kg.) Due to this fact, males are considered to be more manageable in the sport.

Tawny Eagle

The Tawny Eagle, (*Aquila rapax*) is indigenous to India and Africa. Those that originate in Africa tend to be larger and somewhat redder than their Indian relatives.

Because Tawny Eagles fall in a weight range of 2.5-6.6 lbs. / 1.6-3 kg, they are among the easier of the eagles to train, although they can be aggressive if they have imprinted at an early age on humans.

The average length for the species is 24-30 inches / 60-75 cm with a wingspan of 63-75 inches / 159-190 cm. The underparts are tawny with black tail and flight feathers and a pale lower back.

This species can take rabbits and hares with ease, and can be flown in slightly more covered country.

Owls

Many seasoned falconers do not regard the use of eagle owls as true to the tradition of the sport, but these birds are at least worthy of mention as more and more people are starting to train them.

The best option with an owl is to find a hand-reared specimen of about four weeks of age. Adult owls are all but impossible to train.

It should be noted that birds that are completely hand reared from day one will be useless for breeding in the future. Owls left with parents and siblings for the first 3-4 weeks still respond to being tamed, but are also agreeable to breeding later in life.

Allow owls to fly free in their pens at all times. Handle them daily. Some of the species you will see undergoing training include:

- **European Eagle Owl** (*Bubo bubo*), a large owl, with females weighing as much as 7.5 lbs. (3.5 kg). Popular subspecies include: Indian Eagle Owl (*Bubo bubo bengalensis*), Iranian Eagle Owl (*B.b.nikolskii*), Savigny's Eagle Owl (*B.b.ascalaphus*).

- **Great Horned Owl** (*Bubo virginianus*), an aggressive, but somewhat smaller bird ranging from 1.49 to 5.5 lbs. / 0.68 to 5.5 kg.

- **Snowy Owl** (*Nyctea scandiaca*), the only large British Owl, with a reputation for being aggressive to handle. Weighs 3.5-6.6 lbs. / 1.6-3 kgs.

Chapter 3 – Important Questions to Ask Yourself

Falconry is both a sport and an art. The simple definition is that a trained bird of prey is flown at quarry in a wild setting. That, however, is a bit too tidy for a sport that is, at its heart, very fundamental. Make no mistake, falconry is a blood sport, and this is a fact about which you cannot be squeamish and become a falconer.

Can You Kill an Animal?

Perhaps the most important question to ask yourself is simply can you kill? Your hawk may take the quarry, but there is a good chance it will be alive and injured. It will be your job to dispatch the animal.

If you cannot face the prospect of quickly and humanely killing a living creature, you have no business thinking about becoming a falconer for so much as a second.

All of the rest of falconry can be learned. All other challenges can be overcome. But squeamishness at the critical moment of the hunt is non-negotiable. If you can't do what has to be done, don't take up this sport.

Falconry Requires Passionate Interest

If you have been devouring every book you can find on the subject and keeping yourself glued to YouTube videos, you probably have the correct level of interest already. Anything less than passion, however, is not what you want to bring to this all-consuming sport.

In addition to this book, you should also acquire:

- Falconry for Beginners – Lee William Harris
- Falconry and Hawking – Philip Glasier
- Falconry Art and Practice – Emma Ford
- Training Birds of Prey – Jemima Parry-Jones
- Understanding the Bird of Prey – Nick Fox

This is far from an exhaustive list. I highly recommend reading everything you can get your hands on. The more you learn about falconry, the better you will be at discerning good material from bad.

Important Considerations

Other questions to consider include:

- Do you have the time? To fully train your bird, you will need 2-4 hours per day initially for up to three weeks. After that, the bird must be flown daily. Typically birds are flown for 6 months, and then given 6 months in the mews to molt. During that time, your raptor will still need daily interaction and care.

- It is not unusual for a captive raptor to live well into its 20s. While some falconers capture a bird, hunt with it for a time, and release it, many keep their birds for years. Can you meet this considerable commitment to a living creature? Including providing correct and proper housing?

- Do you know an experienced falconer? In some areas (including the United States) you must train with a master falconer to earn your license. At bare minimum, you need someone well versed in the support and care and training of the birds to whom you can turn with questions.

- Are you temperamentally suited to being an apprentice? Can you start at the bottom of your sport knowing you'll stay there for two years or more? If you have to be the best at something the minute you take it up, you may not have the patience for falconry.

- Can you listen to and learn from other people? Can you check your ego at the door and bow to the experience of people more knowledgeable about the sport you are seeking to master?

- Can you afford to get in this game? Although everyone's list of necessary equipment varies, you can assume that you will face an initial investment of $1500-$3000 / £903-£1807 in equipment alone, never mind license and registration fees, the cost of building mews for your bird, and food for the bird, estimated at $1-$3 / £0.60-£1.81 per day.

- Can you face the very real possibility that, at any moment, after all your time and effort, your bird can simply decide to fly away? And that even if the creature is outfitted with telemetry, you may not be able to recover it?

Join a Falconry Organization

If you believe that falconry is indeed a sport at which you, in partnership with a bird, could excel and from which you will derive years of pleasure, then please join a falconry club or similar organization.

Such a group will help you to understand how to obtain training and secure a license (if necessary) in your area, and will also introduce you to the *culture* of the sport. If you find that you can't afford to be a falconer, or that you can't properly house a bird, you can still be involved in falconry as an active advocate and spectator.

(Please see the section at the back of this book called Relevant Websites for partial listings of groups and organization that can be of assistance to beginners.)

Chapter 4 – Overview of Training Procedures

Although there are certainly guiding principles to training a bird of prey, there are many finely nuanced methods for doing so. Needless to say this is a matter of long and vigorous discussion among master falconers.

Truthfully, however, at least in the United States, here are many procedural steps to take first as an apprentice seeks to gain a falconry license. Let's begin with an overview of that journey.

Please note that the following sections were compiled from information provided by the North American Falconers Association (http://www.n-a-f-a.com) and The California Hawking Club (http://www.calhawkingclub.org).

It is imperative that you verify all parts of the application process for your state or province.

Becoming an Apprentice Falconer (US)

The first step in becoming an apprentice falconer is to contact your state or provincial wildlife department or agency. I have provided a list of current web addresses in *Appendix I – State / Provincial Wildlife Agencies.*

(Please note that these addresses were current in mid-2014, but, like all things online, are always subject to change. Also be aware that all attendant registration and license fees for each step of this process vary by state. When you contact your local wildlife department, specifically ask about these fees so you don't get surprised later.)

Request Information

Request information about falconry in the state, including a list of all currently licensed falconers. Also ask for a contact person in your area for a local or state falconry organization. I have attempted to list as many of these as I could find under Relevant Websites at the back of this book, but the list is not comprehensive.

Review and Study

Using the materials provided to you and additional books and manuals you acquire from suggested reading lists, review your commitment to joining the sport and begin to prepare for your written examination. This preparation must include a review and understanding of the federal falconry laws.

Some other steps you may want to take include:

Meeting with an existing falconer for a discussion of the sport and the commitment it requires.

Be aware that most falconers are leery of people who have only a cursory interest in falconry. If you really want to get good information, and perhaps an invitation to go hunting with the falconer, be prepared to illustrate that you are actively studying and learning about the sport.

Attend a meeting of a local or state falconry organization.

Don't just barge in! Call and ask for an invitation, which may be the precursor to the kind of discussion I describe above.

Understand that you are asking admission to a dedicated subculture of people passionate about raptors. Be respectful! None of these people so much as owe you the time of day.

Find a Sponsor

The order in which you acquire a sponsor will differ by region. In some states you will be required to pass your written examination before a sponsor will agree to work with you, in others the sponsor will help you to prepare for the test.

Regardless, you must have a General or Master Class falconer act as your sponsor for a period of two years. Federal regulations require that you be at least 12 years of age, to apply for a falconry license while some states set the minimum age limit higher.

A potential sponsor may ask that you prove your interest and commitment by hunting with them for a period of time *before* they will agree to spend two years working with you. Again, be respectful. You are very much in the "paying your dues" stage of the sport. Accept that.

Pass a Written Exam

The written exam that is required to become a falconer is administered at an office and location stipulated by the game department in your state or province. The test itself is comprised of 100 multiple choice and true/false questions.

Topics covered include the natural history of raptors, their biology, captive care, methods of handling, and healthcare. You will also be expected to know something about the history of falconry as well as the applicable federal and state laws.

A score of 80% is required to pass the test. Most applicants pass on the first attempt, but you are allowed to retake the exam immediately in most cases.

When you receive the results of your test, and provided you have a passing score, you will also receive a falconry license application. This document does require the signature of a sponsor and you will face inspections of both your equipment and the facilities in which you will house your bird.

Hunting License Requirements

In some states you will be required to obtain a hunting license and complete a hunting safety course even though the course is specifically tailored for gun safety. Do not argue the point. If the law requires that you have a hunting license to continue your path to becoming a falconer, comply and get on with it.

Construct Your Mews

By this stage of the process, you should already have a sponsor who will guide you in creating facilities to house your bird that will pass inspection. This is usually done by a game warden who will visit your home. If your facilities do not pass, you can correct the detected flaws and ask for re-inspection, for which a fee is typically charged.

Called by various names, your aviary, mews, or hawk box is typically an 8′ x 8′ x 8′ / 2.44 x 2.44 x 2.44 meter cube. This sufficient for beginner hawk species like the Red-Tailed Hawk (called a Red-tailed Buzzard in the UK.)

For people who cannot have a mews, either due to space considerations or because a governing body like a homeowners association does not permit the construction, it is acceptable for the hawk to be housed elsewhere. This is not, however, an ideal situation.

Your sponsor can help you to consider other alternatives, like converting a room, or constructing a freestanding, portable mews.

Required Equipment

Again, while this may vary slightly by state, you will be required to have jesses, a leash, swivel, outdoor perch, bath pan, and scale capable of reading in half ounce / 14 gram increments. These items will be inspected at the same time your facilities are examined.

Submit Your Application

When your sponsor agrees that both your facilities and your equipment are ready, fill out and submit the license. Shortly thereafter your inspection will be scheduled. If the game warden signs off, you will be ready to trap and train your first bird.

Note that in some states there is an actual trapping season, so some new falconers are forced to wait a period of months before they can acquire their bird.

In the United States when a hawk is caught or transferred you must fill on out a Federal Form 3-186A within 10 days of the capture. You may also be required to fill out additional forms. For instance, in California, a "Resident Falconer Raptor Capture, Recapture and Release Report" is also necessary.

Trapping Your Bird

The bal-chatri trap is a favored method for catching raptors. Some small animal, usually a mouse or rat, is placed inside the trap's cage where the animal is clearly visible as potential prey. The surface of the cage is covered in monofilament nooses that snare the bird's legs.

Once a hawk is caught, the bird's typical reaction is to freeze, especially after a blanket is gently thrown over it. Both bird and trap are carried to a location where the apprentice and master can safely hood the hawk and extricate its legs from the nooses.

The bird is then transported to the darkened mews where a process called "manning" is begun. Although there are many approaches used to accomplish this first stage of the human/bird relationship, I will describe one of the more common methods below.

Manning Your Bird

In training a raptor, you are seeking to forge a working partnership between hawk and falconer created through a program of weight management, positive reinforcement, and repetition. This begins immediately after the bird is captured through an acclimatization process called "manning."

This is the period during which the bird gets used to being around people, becomes particularly comfortable with its handler, and comes to associate food with a signal, typically a whistle, and the falconer's glove.

The easiest approach to manning is to place the newly caught hawk in its mews in the dark. Each time food is offered, the falconer whistles, and then tosses into the mews the food. The highly intelligent hawk quickly comes to associate the sound with being fed.

In Japan and Europe, birds are often kept hooded or in dark rooms so that their handlers can more precisely direct their acclimatization process. This is not unlike the theory behind using blinders with a horse. If the animal does not see anything that is frightening, then there is nothing to be frightened about.

In the U.S., it's more common for the light to be gradually increased in the mews so that the bird can gain an increasing level of confidence in its new surroundings. The process can take as long as a month depending on the individual bird, but the goals are clear.

The bird must be used to your presence, accept you as the provider of food, and be secure in its new environment so that a training regimen can begin.

If you are beginning to work with a captive born bird, the creature will already be accustomed to humans and manning is more a process of getting the hawk comfortable with *you* specifically. Typically such birds can be placed on a bow perch in an open-fronted aviary and allowed to observe their surroundings over a period of about 10 days.

Regardless of the method used, manning requires that the falconer spend hours with the hawk. First food is simply placed in the mews, but then the bird must learn to accept treats on the falconer's glove.

Gradually the bird is taught to step up on the glove to take the food, which sets the stage for the more intimate handling needed to put basic pieces of equipment or "furniture" physically on the hawk.

Again, methods vary. Some falconers choose to place these items on the bird at capture so that adjusting to their presence is part of the broader acclimatization process.

Introducing Basic Equipment

In either case, the next "step" with any hawk is to get the animal used to the basic items of equipment called "furniture" like the hood and, and to teach the animal to sit on your fist and to accept food.

Signal the bird to come to you with the same whistle you used while keeping it isolated in the mews after capture. Attach the leg bells, anklets, and jesses.

- The leg bells, which can alternately be placed on the tail or neck, aid in finding the bird while hunting.

- The anklets are leather straps designed to fit securely around each of the bird's legs and provide an attachment point for the jesses via two brass grommets.

- The jesses are leather straps that allow the falconer to hold the bird and serve as a point of attachment for the leash.

The anklets are left attached at all times, but the bells are sometimes taken off between hunting sessions. Jesses are typically switched out by length and are location dependent. Longer straps are used in the mews or aviary while shorter ones are employed in the field for hunting.

This kind of routine handling, which either involves inspecting or changing out equipment, is also an excellent opportunity to examine the bird's eyes, beak, mouth, legs, feet, talons, wings, feathers, tail, and vent.

I'll discuss more on your bird's health in a separate chapter, but vigilance in spotting and attending to any issues or irregularities on a daily basis is fundamental to good healthcare. Handling also strengthens your bond with the bird and keeps the hawk consistently tame.

If you don't plan to or can't interact with your bird every day, don't take up falconry!

Graduating to the Creance

At the point at which the hawk will jump up on the glove to accept treats, and will allow the falconer to handle it without protest, a creance, which is a line or cord used for training purposes is then introduced.

It is important to only use the creance in an area where it

cannot become tangled in trees or similar obstacles. One end of the creance is always anchored, either to the falconer, or to a weighted creance stick, and the cord is designed to break free under excessive force to protect the bird.

The typical length of a creance is 10 yards / 9.14 meters, but 50 yards / 45.72 meters is employed to verify that the hawk is ready for free flight.

The creance ensures that the falconer remains in control of the hawk as it is taught to hop, jump, and then fly onto the glove for a food reward (in response to the signal whistle) from a series of increasing distances.

When the bird begins to fly to the falconer, a lure is added to the training regimen. It is designed to resemble game the hawk is expected to hunt and is garnished with food to encourage repeated stricks. Larger rewards are given when the hawk comes to the lure, thus reinforcing the desired behavior.

Entering the Bird

Within a month, the bird should be ready to fly freely in pursuit of game. The initial release of the hawk to hunt a given quarry is called "entering." It is a trying time when the hawk may simply fly away and return to its wild life.

For this reason, you should carefully choose the site for entering the bird. It should be an area where the chosen game is in abundance, forcing the bird's native hunting instincts to control its actions.

If the first outing goes smoothly, either the falconer or a companion dog will flush the game on future hunts, which the hawk then chases and kills. The bird is allowed to eat its fill, at which point the falconer approaches and calls the bird onto the glove, rewarding the hawk for its obedience.

The idea is to create clear associations in the mind of the bird with the series of events so that it will repeat its actions on the next outing. The more the falconer and the bird hunt together, the deeper the forging of this bond, which is the heart and soul of the sport.

The Relationship

Falconry works because of the relationship it creates between a highly intelligent wild animal and a human. The hawk sees in the falconer the answer to its most fundamental needs –food, shelter, and healthcare. But at the same time, the human is also a companion in the exercise and hunting the animal instinctually craves.

Once a bird is released to hunt, there is nothing to prevent the hawk from flying away. It is the bond the animal shares with the falconer that causes the animal to return voluntarily time and time again. That return is a sign of both trust and respect, which is why people who fly birds feel such deep emotional ties to them.

Becoming an Apprentice Falconer (UK)

The primary legislation governing birds of prey in the United Kingdom is the Wildlife and Countryside Act of 1981. This law makes it illegal to take, injure or kill any wild bird, or to take, damage or destroy its nest or eggs.

Licenses to capture birds of prey in the wild are no longer issued by the government. The only way you can legally obtain a bird of prey for use in falconry is to purchase a raptor bred in captivity.

Rescuing an injured wild bird to render aid and to release it back into the wild is legal, but if you are caught with such a bird, you will be prosecuted under the presumption of guilt rather than innocence.

If you do take in a bird, contact the Department for Environment, Food & Rural Affairs (DEFRA), the Royal Society for the Prevention of Cruelty to Animals (RSPCA), and the local chapter of the Royal Society for the Protection of Birds (RSPB) to help ensure you do not face legal charges.

Chapter 5 – Equipment or Furniture

In the previous chapter, which provided an overview of becoming an apprentice falconer, the most basic pieces of accoutrement were described. These items barely touch on the recommended equipment or "furniture" the beginning falconer must acquire.

An Area for Your Bird

A raptor's need for an aviary will vary by species. Most beginner's birds (Red-tailed Hawks or Harris Hawks) will do fine in an 8' x 8' x 8' / 2.44 x 2.44 x 2.44 meter cube so long as you interact with the bird and fly it daily.

After all, in nature these birds will assume a high perch and sit motionless for hours. In and around the same area you should have a place to store and work with your equipment as well as weigh your raptor.

Since an arrangement for a mews will vary enormously by circumstance, you may spend as little as $250 / £150 or as much as $1500 / £903.

Scales and Weight Management

Natural predators like raptors only kill to eat. A bird that is well fed to the point of being overweight sees no reason to waste his energy. A bird that is on the poor side can't take the risk of using too much energy.

Falconers have to find the sweet spot in between when the bird is just hungry enough to put in the effort to hunt, but not so empty as to be worried about harming himself.

Weighing the bird at the same time each day, and flying the raptor according to the rhythms of the day helps the falconer to discern an optimum time to be in the field.

For some birds, this is toward evening when they are instinctually concerned about stoking their metabolism to keep their bodies warm through the coming night.

With training, the bird comes to associate the time of day with hunting and regardless of weight, will respond to that programming.

As with many aspects of falconry, there are endless theories about the correct weight at which a bird should be flown. Often, the answer is highly individualistic and must be arrived at by trial and error. Regardless, however, weighing your bird is a huge part of daily care and maintenance in this sport.

Quality digital scales for medium-sized raptors cost around $125 / £75, with those for larger birds starting at $150 / £90 and up.

Glove

The glove or gauntlet is the most readily recognizable of all hawking gear. It, too, can vary by species. Gloves used with falcons typically cover the hand and wrist only, while those used with hawks are much longer, extending up the arm as a true gauntlet. If you are flying an eagle, the glove covers almost the entire arm.

Traditionally, falconers wear the glove on the left hand, but clearly this is reversed for left-handers. The purpose of the glove is not only to protect you, but also to give the bird a secure perch.

You should condition the glove in advance to prevent it from becoming soaked with blood. Use a high-quality product like Pecard's Leather Care or NurtureSeal. Both are available for approximately $15 / £9 per 4 ounces / 113.4 grams.

It is important not to allow the glove leather to become stiff and brittle. In addition to the initial conditioning, the glove should be cleaned regularly with antibacterial soap or a solution of warm water and 10% bleach.

Scrub out all dried material (bits of meat and blood) lodged in the seams and in any crevices or cracks. Allow the glove to dry thoroughly and then use the leather treatment again.

Some falconers cannot afford to have a glove custom made to a tracing of their hand, which are available in a price range of $75-$200 / £45-£120. These individuals often opt to use welding gloves instead, at a cost of approximately $15 / £9 per pair.

If you go this route, modify the glove to include a D-ring onto which the bird's jesses can be secured.

Bells

Two bells are attached to birds to help in locating the creatures during hunting. Some falconers leave the bells in place at all times, others take them on and off the bird in between outings.

Bells should be chosen not just for their loudness relative to their size, but also for the comfort of the falcon. Use only bells specifically designed for the sport of falconry.

Bells are either attached to the anklets, or placed on the tail or around the neck.

The best quality bells are made of either brass or bronze, and are often available in a two-tone combination which makes them easier to hear at a distance. Depending on size and configuration, most bells are priced in a range of $20-$30 / £12-£18.

Bewits

The small leather strips used to attach bells to a bird's legs are called bewits. Only leather should be used to attach any kind of equipment to the bird in such a way that it is coming into direct contact with the skin. Most bewits, even when cut to order, cost only around $5 / £3.

Anklets

The anklets also come into contact with the bird's leg and remain in place for extended periods of time. They should be safe and comfortable. There may be subtle differences in design, but the preferred material is kangaroo leather. Basically, the anklet is an elongated leather oval with two round holes in each end. When the leather is wrapped around the bird's leg, the anklet is joined together with a brass grommet.

It is quite common for falconers to make their own anklets, but in the beginning, you may want to purchase anklets and use them as a template.

If you do acquire your own leather from which you will cut future sets of anklets, make sure it is vegetable tanned and contains nothing that will irritate the bird's skin.

From a falconry supply store, a set of kangaroo leather anklets costs less than $8 / £5.

Jesses

Jesses may be made of leather, parachute cord, or other material and can also be braided. They are straps that are passed through the grommets in the anklets and held there by a button or knot that serves as a stop.

On the opposite end, the jesses are notched for the insertion of a swivel, which in turn attaches to the leash.

Longer "mews" jesses are used for birds in their aviary, while shorter "field" jesses are used for training or hunting.

Again, this is an item that a falconer can make, but if purchased, and depending on length and strength (varies by species), a pair of jesses will range from $8-$15 / £5-£9.

Swivels

Beginners should have 2 or more swivels on hand. These small metal joints are affixed between the leash and jesses to prevent tangling. Especially when the bird is on the perch, this is crucial to keep the hawk from injuring itself.

There are several different types of swivels (barrel, ball, coastlock, v-shaped, and so on.) Size and weight needed vary by species. Small swivels cost approximately $5 / £3, while those for larger species may be $30 / £18.

Leashes

Traditionally crafted from leather, the leash attaches the bird to the perch or to the falconer's glove. There are many variations and a variety of materials employed,
Modern leashes have taken many forms, but most retail for well under $30 / £18.

Hood

Hoods are used in falconry to keep the birds calm. Birds do not become alarmed about what they cannot see. This is an Arabic contribution to the sport, brought to Europe during the Crusades. Today the best hoods are made of kangaroo hide.

Obviously hoods are sized according to species, with the

design accommodating the contour of the eyes. Sizing is done by measuring across the top of the hood looking down. A female Harris Hawk or a male Red-Tailed Hawk will measure approximately 2.3 inches / 5.84 cm.

There are many regional styles, some quite elaborate. As a result, prices vary widely in a range of $65-$100 / £40-£60 - or more.

Bow or Bow Perch

A bow perch is a rounded perching surface the bird can grip completely with its talons. To purchase one in the correct size for a Harris or Red-Tailed hawk, expect to pay around $130-$150 / £78-£90.

Note that depending on where you house and train the bird, you may wind up with one or more of these perches. For this reason, many falconers opt for the "do it yourself" approach.

The surface chosen for the perch is critical to the health of the raptor's feet as is the state in which the surface is maintained.

Many modern falconers use Astroturf because it is both soft and easy to clean, while others prefer to wrap the surface tightly in hemp rope.

Bath

Like all birds, raptors need to be able to get into water and soak. This is an important aspect of husbandry and a requirement for healthy feathers. A bath of the correct size for a hawk or falcon costs less than $20 / £12.

Hawking Bag or Jacket

Whether you go into the field keeping the items you need, including meat, in a hawking bag or jacket is up to you.

All-leather traditional hawking bag retail for $100-$150 / £60-£90. This is a good investment, however, as such bags typically contain a removable and washable pouch for meat.

Smaller bags with less storage typically cost less than $75 / £45. Hawking jackets start in the $90 / £54 range.

Lure

Dummy bags or lures are created by taking a padded form with a cord attached ($25-$35/£15-£21) and augmenting it to look like the bird's intended quarry for training purposes.

Adding a rabbit fur to the lure or a pair of pheasant wings adds about $10 / £6 to the overall price of the creation.

Creance and Creance Stick

For all practical purposes a creance is simply a longer leash, but one end is always anchored, either to the falconer, or to a weighted tube. The creance is used to train the bird for longer free flight sessions before entering it against intended quarry.

A 50-yard/ 45.72-meter length of creance with a tube attached can be purchased for $35 / £21.

Telemetry System

Most falconers today use some form of radio telemetry to track and recover their birds. With some species this is more necessary than with others, but for any falconer, placing a transmitter on the bird is a distinct advantage.

A quality telemetry receiver with a folding antenna retails for approximately $500 / £300. Transmitters are available from $150 / £90 and up.

Travel Box

As the name implies, travel boxes are used to safely transport your hawk. A large travel box for a single bird will measure approximately 17 inches / 43.18 cm wide by 20 inches / 50.8 cm deep x 24 inches / 60.96 cm tall. Such a box from a retail source will cost approximately $85.00 / £51.24.

Custom-made travel boxes are sold in a range of $125-$240 / £75-£145.

Estimated Costs

Without factoring in the application fees that will be part of the process, and using only the minimum and maximum figures from the previous pages, a beginner can easily spend $1500 / £903 to $3000 / £1807 to become involved in and outfitted for life as a falconer.

Having said that, however, there are many pieces of equipment that falconers can and do fabricate themselves. If you are working with a master falconer who can instruct you in the correct way to make these items, your entry level costs and ongoing costs may be much lower over time.

There is also considerable variance in the costs of constructing an aviary or mews for your falcon. If you are able to do the work yourself and will be out nothing more than the cost of material, this will also be a huge savings.

The cost of feeding a hawk per day is typically estimated to be $1-$3 / £0.60-£1.81.

Chapter 6 – Health and Ongoing Maintenance

Perhaps one of the greatest challenges you will face in managing the long-term health of your bird is finding a qualified avian veterinarian that has experience treating raptors.

In many instances, such professionals are associated with colleges of veterinary medicine or raptor rehabilitation centers. Always factor in the potential need to travel some distance to get your bird the care it needs.

To begin your search for a vet in the United States, visit the website for the Association of Avian Veterinarians at http://www.abvp.org or check the listings maintained by the California Hawking Club at http://www.calhawkingclub.org.

In the UK, contact the Falcon Veterinary Group at falconvet.co.uk (physical office at 330 London Road, Carlisle, Cumbria, CA1 3ER, telephone 01228 558833.)

Know Your Bird

In order to be able to describe to an avian veterinarian or other knowledgeable person what is wrong with your raptor, you must be intimately familiar with the bird not only in a behavioral sense, but also anatomically.

Throughout the following chapter I will refer to various parts of the raptor's body, and more terms are included in Chapter 7 – Learning to Speak "Falconry." Clearly during your apprenticeship you will be working with and handling birds, but I heartily recommend having a good reference source on hand like:

- Practical Handbook of Falconry Husbandry and Medicine by Margit Gabriele Muller, Nova Science Publishers, 2009.

Reference sources are especially important for falconers living at a good distance from qualified avian veterinarians, or those forced to work with vets who have very little if any experience with raptors.

Overview of Basic Anatomy

The following material is intended as an overview of the basics of avian anatomy. It is not comprehensive, but does cover the major external features.

Head

- Starting in the corner of the mouth there is a very delicate area of skin called the *commisure*.

- Moving up along the beak, you will find the *tomial notch*, which matches the second hook on a raptor's beak. In the absence of actual teeth, these two structures form a crushing point for breaking the neck of a prey animal.

- Above the beak is an area called *operculum* or *cere*. It is an area of smooth, featherless skin.

- The *external nostrils* are also located at the top of the bill and vary in shape by species.

- The *supraorbital ridge* or brow bone sits above the eye. In immature birds, it will be poorly developed.

- The *forehead* is the area from the base of the upper mandible (jaw) to a line roughly through the middle of the eyes.

- The top of the head lying behind the forehead and extending to the first cervical vertebrae in the neck is the *crown*.

- The area at the base of the neck is the *nape*.

- The *eye ring* is a grouping of feathers around the eye that often contrast with the adjacent plumage.

- Many birds of prey also have an *eye line*, which extends along the side of the head away from the eye. Both the eye ring and eye line are useful marks in identifying a species, as is the color of the *iris*, and of the *pupil* of the eye itself.

Wing

- The collective term for the flight feathers is *remiges*. They attach to the bone and are long and stiff.

- The *primary feathers* attach to the *"manus"* or hand, which is the outermost skeletal structure of the wing. They provide the main force of propulsion during flight. In most species there are 11 primary feathers.

- The *secondary feathers* are attached to the *ulna*, which is the middle skeletal structure of the wing. These feathers provide a large surface area for soaring.

- The group of three small, stiff feathers that arise from the first digit of the hand act as an aerodynamic slot to control air flow over the wing during flight. They are called the *alula*.

- The *coverts* overlay the alula and the remiges on both the dorsal and ventral surface and are named according to location.

- The *scapular feathers* arise at the shoulder and often cover most of the wing when the bird is perched. Their corollaries on the ventral side are the *axillary feathers*.

Tail

- The paired flight feathers on the tail are called the *retrices*. There are typically 12. They act as a rudder to steer the bird while in flight.

- The *tail coverts* cover the base of the retrices. The upper coverts blend into the rump, but the undertail coverts are called the *crissum* and are more distinctive.

Feet

- Hunting birds like hawks and falcons have *anisodactyl* feet, meaning there are three toes forward and one back.

- The toe that points toward the back is called the *hallux*, and in hawks is the primary weapon used to puncture the vital organs of prey animals.

- The hallux is considered the "first" toe. Moving clockwise, the remaining toes are 2, 3, and 4.

- The *raptorial foot* found in birds of prey is characterized by the presence of heavy claws or *talons* used for catching, holding, and killing prey.

Body

- The *keel* is the sternum or breastbone, which sits vertically in the chest. Using your thumb and forefinger on either side of the keel, you can judge the health of the bird in terms of muscle density. There should be barely any bone detectable in a healthy, well fed bird.

- The *vent* is the external surface under the tail that houses the *cloaca*. This single external opening is where fecal matter is expelled and urine passed, and is also the location of the genital tract. This area should always be clean and dry.

Signs of a Healthy Bird

Healthy birds are actively engaged with their environment, showing both interest and energy. They will preen and bathe regularly.

The bird will bate at times, meaning it will attempt to fly from its perch or from the falconer's fist while still attached to the leash. This often occurs because the hawk has seen something of interest, or is anxious to go hunting.

Birds in good condition also rouse, which is the action of erecting and shaking the feathers as an aspect of grooming. This is a sign that you have a contented and relaxed hawk.

Normal behavior is comprised of a degree of balance, ranging from attacking food with relish to reacting with a degree of uncertainty over new environmental elements.

Individuals will have their own quirks. For instance some birds tuck their heads under their wings to sleep, while others lie down. Learn what is normal *for your bird* and make your health assessments accordingly.

With any bird, however, the following symptoms are indicative of possible problems:

- listlessness or lethargy
- puffy or enlarged eyes
- pronounced changes in appetite or feeding behavior
- offensive smelling fecal matter (mutes)

You are the best judge of your hawk's behavior. If you think something is wrong, it probably is. Do not hesitate to seek the help of a veterinary professional. Birds can sicken and die very quickly, especially when they begin to lose weight. Do not put your raptor at risk out of fear that you will seem overly anxious or be perceived as an alarmist.

Evaluating Mutes and Castings

The term "mute" refers both to the fecal matter of a raptor and to the act of defecation. Examining the consistency and appearance of mutes and castings (the undigested bits of prey including bones and fur a raptor regurgitates) can provide useful information about the bird's overall well-being.

Mutes rang in consistency from loose to the point of being watery to a kind of chalky powder. They may be tan or tarry black, and be deposited as pellets or "goo."

If there is green material present, the bird is passing bile, indicating the raptor's weight is low. What the bird is eating will also affect the appearance of the mutes. Too much rabbit meat, for instance, and the bird will appear to be passing soft chalk.

Small specks of red may indicate the presence of coccidiosis. Watery gray to greenish mutes can point to parasite activity. (Strong smelling fecal matter almost certainly confirms a parasite infestation.)

Clearly castings will vary based on the food consumed, but the real point is to make sure your raptor *is* casting. If undigested material is not coming up routinely, your bird may be in danger of suffering an impaction.

Parasites

Your raptors can be affected by any number of external and internal parasites, most of which are easy enough to treat. This is not indicative of poor husbandry, but often occurs as a consequence of consuming or coming into contact with prey that is already infested.

Lice

Lice are small white, worm-like parasites that may be visible crawling around the vent. They lay their eggs along the shafts of the feathers.

To cure the infestation, spray the bird with a Pyrethrin solution, repeating as necessary in 10 days to catch any newly emerged lice.

Ticks

Ticks can be very difficult to detect without magnification, but are easily removed from your raptors with poultry dust or any 0.25% Permethrin powder. Besides removing the insects may be necessary if the bites become infected.

Worms

Raptors living with a low level infestation of worms may refuse slips (refuse to fly at prey), exhibit general lethargy, pass foul-smelling feces, and experience delayed molting.

Vets are in agreement that birds should be wormed at the time they are trapped, with a secondary treatment in two weeks. The birds should then be tested annually, and wormed at the end of each hunting season.

Panacur is a favored drug for this purpose and is either placed in the crop via a small tube or injected in a piece of meat. Please note that only a qualified veterinarian should administer the medication directly into the crop.

Stargazing Syndrome

Birds with Stargazing Syndrome are suffering from Vitamin B1 deficiency that causes inflammation of the brain. They are in need of more whole food in their diet and require the administration of raptor-specific vitamins.

The symptomatic behavior in Stargazing Syndrome is clear and pronounced. The bird will stand and stare at the ceiling or pull its head backwards over the shoulders.

Treating External Injuries

A vet's services will be required if your raptor is suffering from a talon wound inflicted by another bird, or has been bitten by a prey animal fighting to save its life. This is especially common with some types of quarry like squirrels, necessitating the use of protective leg gear for the hawk.

Scratches and scrapes that are often a consequence of hunting can typically be treated with Neosporin ointment, but wounds that may be subject to infection will require amoxicillin.

Be vigilant in examining the area around the mouth. Birds are sometimes cut when they consume bones. These small abrasions can easily become inflamned if other particles of food become lodged in the wound.

Bumblefoot

Injuries to your bird's feet are especially worrisome since even the smallest corn on a raptor's foot can turn into a painful, inflamed swelling called Bumblefoot. This will cause the hawk to lay down and take any other means necessary not to put weight on the affected foot.

The best prevention against bumblefoot is good nutrition and the maintenance of proper and sanitary perching surfaces. In addition to being clean, perches should also be offered in a variety of sizes to encourage more exercise of the feet and thus to improve blood flow.

Use natural materials as perch coverings such as sisal, bark, cork, or cocoa mats. Avoid anything that has been chemically treated or that contains formaldehyde. Remove or file down all sharp surfaces in the bird's habitat to lessen the chance of injury.

(Although some falconers swear by it, the use of Astroturf as a perching surface remains controversial.)

To treat bumblefoot when it does occur, the affected area must be cleaned and treated with an antibiotic. Under ideal circumstances, a veterinarian will then be enlisted to remove any corns that are present to prevent a recurrence of the painful irritation.

As regular maintenance, scrub your raptor's feet with antibacterial soap using a soft toothbrush. Take your time on the underside to ensure the area is free of any dried meat residue and blood. Pay particular attention to crevices where such materials can lodge.

Afterward the feet have been thoroughly cleaned, massage in a small amount of an avian-specific foot salve, or mix your own by combining equal parts of anhydrous lanolin and Dermaclense.

Other Abnormalities of the Mouth / Neck

Hawks are susceptible to **trichomoniasis,** a highly contagious yeast infection of the digestive tract. Raptors contract the condition from eating infected birds, especially pigeons.

The invading organism is a flagellated protozoan that infiltrates the sinuses, mouth, throat, esophagus, and other organs.

The resulting lesions, which are flat and filled with cheesy pus may be most evident in the mouth. Successful treatments include metronidazole and dimetridazole.

(Avian Trichomoniasis is commonly called **Frounce**.)

Also watch for swellings on the side of the throat, which should not be dismissed as a full crop. The bird could have an **infected salivary gland,** which will be evident if you look down the hawk's throat.

A veterinarian must clear the plug of pus with subsequent antibiotic treatment administered.

If the crop is bulging and the bird's breath is bad, it can be suffering from *sour crop*, which often results from the use of an antibiotic to resolve another illness, or from over-feeding an underweight or otherwise weakened bird.

Sour crop should be resolved by giving the bird Pedialyte. This will keep the hawk hydrated while flushing the crop. If, however, there is no improvement in 8 hours, consult your veterinarian.

Respiratory Illnesses

Aspergillosis is a fungal infection of the respiratory tract. The major symptoms are labored or shallow breathing and wheezing with the inability to vocalize or a change in the sound/quality of the vocalization. The usual treatments are Ancobon (flucytosine) or Amphotericin B.

In some cases, a secondary bacterial infection, typically pneumonia will develop in the lower respiratory tract necessitating the use of antibiotics.

In order to guard against cases of aspergillosis, keep your bird's quarters clean and well ventilated.

Clear and watery nasal discharge, especially around meal times is normal, but if you see a milky, white or globby discharge, be sure to have your hawk evaluated for an infection, especially if there is accompanying swelling around the eyes.

Coping the Beak

Captive raptors require our help in keeping their beaks appropriately maintained and well-shaped, a process in wild birds that occurs naturally when they break the bones of their prey and work the meat loose.

Unless you are highly experienced and have a clear sense of the correct shape of the bird's upper and lower beak, seek the help of a more experienced falconer or a veterinary professional in accomplishing this maintenance task.

Optimally, the job should be done with a power tool like a Dremel (with extreme caution taken in regard to heat build up.) Do not use a tool of this sort if you don't know what you're doing! The risk of seriously injuring the bird is simply too great.

Metal files are also employed, and are safer for those falconers less experienced with this chore. For some parts of the procedure, it will be necessary to hold the bird's mouth open with the handle of a wooden spoon or a similar implement.

Coping the beak is a highly stressful chore for the bird due to the noise and the threatening motions. If not handled correctly, the bird can be severely disfigured or injured. Do not attempt this process without expert assistance!

Coping the Talons

In captivity, it is not unusual for birds to develop spiraled talons. Re-shaping or coping with a Dremel tool or file corrects the problem and encourages correct growth. Some birds will stand quietly and allow this work without protest, while others must be cast (held down).

While the talons are being coped, check the point at which the hard structure meets the flesh of the foot. This is a prime location for infection to develop. Warning signs include red lines or spots.

Corns will have a more natural color, but will be raised and hard like a wart. Your veterinarian should remove such protuberances to guard against instances of bumblefoot.

Maintaining Your Bird's Living Area

There is no getting around the fact that all birds, and most especially raptors, are messy. You will be faced with the constant challenge of keeping your bird and its area clean.

The best disinfecting solution is derived from mixing one cup of bleach per gallon of water to achieve an approximate 5% bleach solution.

An alternative is swimming pool chlorine at a concentration of one cup per 2 gallons of water for regular cleaning, and one cup per one gallon for tougher jobs.

Any item to be cleaned should be allowed to soak in the solution. Rinse all items and surfaces thoroughly and allow them to sit in the sun for at least a day before they are put back in with the bird.

Neither solution is good for getting left over grease from meat fat off surfaces, which will require liquid laundry detergent or a household cleaner like Spic N Span. The product has four surfactants to reduce the surface tension of the grease including sodium xylenesulfonate, nonoxynol-9, cocamidopropyl betaine, and coconut fatty acid.

Although power washing is often used to get mutes and other dirt off surfaces and out of travel boxes, the spray sends bacteria and fecal matter into the air.

Wear a facemask while working with the washer, and do not reintroduce the bird to the area for several hours.

Nutritional Overview

Proper nutrition is the bedrock of good health for your birds. What you feed a captive raptor should be a balanced re-creation of what the creature would eat in the wild.

Dietary needs vary by species.

Not all raptors can be fed in the same way. A Red-Tailed Hawk will do very well on a diet of rabbit, rat, and pigeon with the occasional offering of quail and beef heart, but this would not be the correct mixture for a Sharp-Shinned Hawk or a Gyrfalcon.

Know what your specific bird should eat.

The following dietary fundamentals hold true for feeding all captive birds:

- Variety is important to ensure the correct mix of nutrients, and foods should be regularly rotated.

- Know how your feed animals are themselves being fed. A malnourished rat or pigeon will not provide good quality nutrition for your bird.
- Do not attempt to strip all fat from the bird's diet. Some fat content is necessary for healthy feathers.

- Bones are a necessary part of your bird's diet for mineral content. Even indigestible bones are essential to keep the crop clean.

- Never feed frozen or hot foods. Defrost items thoroughly and serve them at a temperature that is warm to the touch. Thawing foods in a warm water bath is perfect for achieving both goals and will prevent the growth of bacteria.

- Do not defrost food with a microwave as it heats the items unevenly.

- Do not use processed or cooked foods.

There are many theories about how much food any raptor should receive relative to its weight and level of activity. There are no hard and fast rules.

Designing a diet for your bird should be an individualized process that meets the needs of the bird and supports the level of its specific activity.

Apprentices are encouraged to consult with a master falconer to design an optimal nutritional program.

Field First Aid Fundamentals

Every falconer should have an avian first aid kit that goes with them into the field. If possible, take an avian medical reference with you as well, and all contact information for your veterinarian, including an emergency number.

Note: The following information is an overview of basic first aid for selected potential injuries. It is not a replacement for proper veterinary care.

Hunting birds can face all manner of field injuries, including attack by other animals, cuts from barbed wire or other fencing, or collisions with vehicles or immovable objects.

Typically it does take two people to restrain and care for an injured bird. All parties involved must stay very calm. Birds pick up on emotions and will panic if their handlers panic.

Emergency Feeding

Diet and proper nutrition is so critical to a bird's survival, that every first aid kit should include provisions for emergency feeding.

A good mix includes all the following in equal parts:

- meat flavored baby food
- corn syrup or honey
- Pedialyte
- one or two egg yolks
- a small pinch of salt
- 0.5 cc liquid avian vitamins

Warm to body temperature and place in the bird's mouth with an eyedropper or a syringe with the needle removed.

Be sure to keep the bird warm to facilitate digestion. Continue to feed the bird every 2-3 hours until veterinary assistance is procured. Do not overfeed or force feed.

Bleeding Injuries

Avian blood has few clotting agents. A broken blood feather can cause blood loss sufficient to kill a healthy bird.

- Clean the area with rubbing alcohol or betadine, but do *not* use hydrogen peroxide.

- Apply pressure with sterile gauze.

- Use a clotting gel or cornstarch, baking soda or flour, but *not* silver nitrate.

- Pack the site liberally with styptic.

If the bleeding is from a feather, apply cornstarch or flour to the shaft. Tissue glue is better if available, but care must be taken not to get the material on surrounding feathers.

If bleeding from a broken blood feather cannot be stopped and you cannot get the bird to a vet, take hold of the shaft of the feather at the base close to the skin with needle-nose pliers or a hemostat. Holding the wing firmly, quickly pull out the shaft and apply pressure to the follicle for at least 1 minute with your thumb and forefinger. If necessary, apply cornstarch or flour.

If the feather is broken off, but not bleeding, *do not* pull the feather! There is a good chance you will damage the folicle. All bleeding injuries in birds should be treated as an emergency. Seek the aid of a veterinarian as quickly as possible.

If the bleeding is from the vent, you have a **serious emergency**. Keep the bird warm and quiet and get to a vet quickly.

Broken Bones

In cases of obvious fracture, wrap the bird in a stocking so that it does not flap its wings or split the broken bone. If a bone end is exposed, slather with a glycerin based gel or Neosporin. This may save the bone from amputation.

Broken Beak

Keep the bird still and apply styptic to the area after gently patting it clean with gauze. If the bleeding does not stop in just a few minutes, get the bird to the vet. Broken beaks can be treated with dental acrylic or methyl methacrylate, which is used to repair broken hooves in horses.

Collisions

In raptors, collisions are typically head on. Both the cranium and the keel may be damaged. It is not unusual for the bird to be unconscious after such an accident.

Gently pick up the bird, being careful to keep it in the same position in case broken bones are present. Wrap the bird in a towel for transport and get to the vet.

Summary

Clearly this is not a comprehensive list of potential injuries in the field, but an overview of some of the more common ones. Again, as part of being a responsible falconer, acquire a raptor-specific medical reference book and study the material.

Chapter 7 – Learning to Speak "Falconry"

Rather than including a traditional glossary at the end of this book, I have decided to provide an entire chapter of falconry terms. Falconry is more a lifestyle in many ways than it is a sport. There is a unique sub-culture associated with flying birds, one that is heavily terminology reliant.

Not all of these terms are actually used in the text of this book, but I assure you that in a room full of falconers, you will hear these and many more. At first, you'll have no earthly idea what anyone is talking about!

Aba – The cloth used for purposes of immobilization to keep a bird calm while it is being examined or otherwise worked with.

Aerie – The nesting place of a raptor, typically in a high location, for instance a cliff.

Alula – A trio of three small and stiff feathers positioned to control the flow of air over the wing when the bird is flying.

Anklets – Anklets are leather straps placed around the bird's legs and to which the jesses are attached. Each anklet may sometimes be referred to as a bracelet.

Austringer – The correct terminology for a "shortwinger" or "dirt hawker" who flies short-wing or broad-wing hawks.

Bal Chatri – A bal chatri is a traditional trap widely used by individuals who capture birds for rehabilitation or training. It is often referred to as a "BC." It is both safe and simple, being comprised of a small cage in which live bait is placed, and a surface covered in monofilament nooses designed to ensnare the bird's toes.

Band – An identification ring made of plastic or metal placed around a bird's legs. Banding is required in some parts of the United States, especially for birds bred in captivity.

Bate – A raptor is said to bate when it attempts to fly from the perch or the fist while still attached to the leash. This may be a reaction to having been startled, an expression of curiosity, or impatience to hunt.

Bathe – Birds bathe when they soak their feathers in a bedpan of water, which is an important part of good raptor husbandry. Soaking is crucial for the health of the bird's feathers.

Beak – A bird's beak is the structure comprised of keratin that covers the mouth and protects the tongue. Raptors have hooked beaks.

Bechin – Refers to a very small morsel or tidbit of food.

Bells – Bells are attached to the bird's feet, neck, or tail as an aid in finding the raptor when it is hidden in trees or brush.

Bewit – The small leather strips used primarily to attach bells (but also other hardware) to a raptor's legs are called bewits.

Bind – Bind means to grab and hold. A bird may bind the falconer's hand, the quarry itself, or a lure.

Block Perch – A block perch is the traditional form used for a falcon and resembles a stool, usually with a pedestal and a rounded top.

Blood Feathers – Blood Feathers are those that continue to grow and therefore are receiving a supply of blood via the shaft.

Bloom – Feathers with "bloom" have a healthy sheen showing that the bird is being well maintained and fed. Feathers that "bloom" and are in peak condition are also waterproof.

Bob Up-and-Down – When raptors exhibit this distinctive head movement, they are communicating interest and may well be judging the distance to an object.

Bow Net – A bow net is another form of trap that, when set, appears to be a circle lying on the ground. When the bird springs the trap, the circle releases, sending a semi-circular bag of net over the raptor, ensnaring it.

Bow Perch - The traditional perch for a hawk, which provides a curved, covered surface on which the raptor sits.

Bowse – "Bowse" is a term meaning "to drink."

Braces – The leather straps on a raptor's hood that are used to open and close the covering are called the braces.

Brail – A brail is a leather thong used to make it impossible for a raptor to bate, especially while the bird is being manned.

Brancher – Branchers are immature birds that have developed their pinfeathers but have not yet flown, they can only jump from one branch to the next.

Break In – The term "break in" means the raptor immediately tears into the catch and starts to eat.

Button – The folded or knotted end of the jess that stops the material against the anklet, or the braided end of the leash is called either a "button" or a "knurl."

Cadge – A cadge is a frame that is used as a perch so that several birds may be carried at one time.

Cast – There are multiple definitions of the word cast in falconry. A bird is said to cast when it regurgitates undigested portions of food. Cast can also refer to the process of holding a bird down so that the creature may be examined or worked with in some way. Finally, the word also refers to a group of birds that are flown and hunting together, as in a pack.

Cast Away – Although the term is used rarely, it is a reference to a raptor's vomiting of undigested material from the crop and stomach.

Cast Off – This is the action taken by the falconer to push the bird off the fist and send it airborne.

Casting -- The casting is the actual mass of undigested (and indigestible) matter regurgitated by a bird of prey, typically consisting of fur and bone among other materials.

Cere – A bird's cere is that area of smooth skin on which there are no feathers that sits just above the beak toward the forehead. It is also referred to as the operculum.

Chaps – Chaps are protection for a bird's legs that are put in place when the raptor hunts certain prey, primarily squirrels, that may severely injure the bird's legs with bites as they fight for their lives.

Choanal Slit – The choanal slit is located in the roof of the bird's mouth and connects to the sinuses.

Cloaca – The external opening on a bird's body through which fecal matter is expelled is the cloaca. It is a single opening from which both fecal matter and urine are passed and where the genital tract is located.

Commissure – The commissure is a very delicate point at the corner of a bird's mouth that can be easily cut or injured.

Coping – Coping is the process by which a bird's beak is re-shaped to achieve optimal form. The same term can also be used for the trimming and shaping of a bird of prey's talons.

Coverts – The "coverts" are a row of feathers that run down the wing over the primary and secondary feathers. There are other covert feathers located on the body, including those on the tail and over the alulas.

Crab – When two birds "crab," they fight or scuffle over a catch, each seeking to gain control and "break in" the quarry in order to feed.

Creance – The creance is a long line used for training purposes with one end always attached either to the falconer or to a weight. It is used in the initial free flight tests before a bird is ready to be flown on its own with the reasonable expectation that it will return to the glove.

Crines – The short feathers around the cere and beak that appear to be hair-like in nature are called "crines."

Crop – A bird's crop is a pouch, located on the esophagus, where food is softened and separated before being passed on to the stomach.

Crouch – When a bird of prey lowers its body and extends the wings slightly in anticipation of taking flight, the action is said to be a "crouch."

Crural – The crural feathers are those that cover a bird's upper leg to the abdomen. In some species, this covering extends to the top of the foot.

Deck – The term deck refers to the two center tail feathers.

Dho-gazza – A dho-gazza trap employs a net that is suspended between the bait and the bird. When the bird flies into the net, it collapses and entangles the raptor. This can be a highly stressful means of catching a bird since extricating it from the net can be quite difficult.

Draw the Braces - To draw the braces means to pull the straps of a raptor's hood so that they tighten and are drawn closed.

Ear – Although there is virtually no external evidence of the fact, raptors, like all birds, have ear openings on each side of the head that are typically covered by feathers.

Enseam – The process of bringing a raptor out of molt with managed nutrition, weight control, and exercise is called "enseam." If manning it to be done after the molt, the process may be referred to as "reclaim."

Enter – To "enter" a bird is to introduce it to specific quarry while hunting with the falconer. Even if the bird has taken the game in the wild, the animal is not "entered" until the experience occurs in the company of the handler.

Eyass – A baby raptor, still in down, with no pinfeathers is called an eyass. The term may also be used to refer to a bird that was taken from the nest while it was still a downy chick.

Feak – Feak is the action of rubbing the beak against a surface to clean it. Feaking is an indication of contentment.

Fledgling – A fledgling is a bird that, although immature, has flown at least once, but remains under the care of adult birds and is still not fully in control of its flight ability.

Foot – A raptor is said to "foot" when it grabs on to something with the foot and talons, especially the lure or the quarry during a hunt. To foot also describes an aggressive striking out at the falconer's hand

Free Loft – Birds that are allowed free loft can roam fully in their mews without being tethered. Not all birds adapt well to this additional freedom and may not be safe under these circumstances.

Fret Marks – When a bird is sick or starved while its feathers are growing, stress marks called "fret marks" form across the feathers themselves. This may also be called stress bars, shock marks, hunger streaks, or hunger traces.

Full Summed – A bird is full summed when it has reached the end of the molt and sports a complete new set of feathers.

Gape – The term "gape" refers to the width of a bird's oral opening when measured from corner to corner.

Gauntlet – "Gauntlet" is an alternate term for the falconer's glove, which is worn traditionally on the left hand. The length of the glove varies by species flown. For some of the larger birds, like eagles, the glove may indeed cover most of the arm like a full gauntlet.

Glottis - The glottis is a valve located at the base of the tongue. Its purpose is to close the trachea to prevent food or liquid from entering the breathing tube.

Gorge - To gorge a bird is to allow the raptor to eat as much as it likes in one meal. This is generally a reward for an unusually fine effort hunting, or for making a huge forward step in a training regimen.

Hack - To hack is to give a bird the freedom to come and go while the falconer still provides food and shelter. This practice is typically used with immature birds being raised without imprinting. Just before the birds leave on migration or begin to hunt on their own they will be trapped.

Also a soft release method of returning a bird to the wild.

Haggard -- A haggard is a wild bird in full adult plumage that has reached the age of one year or more.

Hallux – The hallux is the toe of a raptor that points backwards. In hawks, the hallux talon is largely responsible for puncturing the vitals of prey animals. The hallux is technically considered to be the first toe.

Halsband – "Halsband" is the German word for a "jangoli," which is a leather strap looped around a raptor's neck and hung down as an aid in propelling the bird. Used mainly with hawks.

Hard Penned – The term "hard penned" refers to a feather shaft when the blood supply has rescinded, indicating the feather is no longer growing. The base of the feather appears white. The phrase "hard penned" may also be used in reference to the bird itself.

Hawk Box – A hawk box is a ventilated box designed to hold a raptor for travel. It may also be referred to as a "giant hood."

Hood – The hood used with raptors is a leather covering for the head, which prevents the creature from seeing external stimuli that would prove overwhelming or frightening and touch off potentially harmful or uncontrollable reactions.

Imp – To imp is to cut the shaft of a broken feather and to glue a replacement feather of the correct length in place.

Imprint – When humans raise raptors rather than the birds being reared by their own kind, the birds come to identify with the humans, imprinting on them, which is often the foundation for inappropriate behavior and aggression.

Intermew – An intermewed bird is one that has molted while in captivity.

Jangoli – A jangoli is a leather strap looped around the bird's neck and then hung down to help propel the bird. They are used primarily with hawks and may also be referred to as a halsband.

Jerkin - A "jerkin" is a male Gyrfalcon.

Jess – Jesses are strips of leather attached to grommets in the anklets to provide a means for the falconer to hold the bird for attaching the leash. Modern jesses are also made out of various braided materials and parachute cord.

Jess Extender – The jess extender servers to combine the jesses into a single unit and connects the swivel to the leash for a more tangle-free tethering method.

Jokin – The term "jokin" is used in the UK for birds that are sleeping. Adults can simply sleep while standing, but most tuck their heads beneath their wings.

Keel – The keel of a bird is the sternum, a large bone lying vertically in the breast. By placing the keel between the thumb and forefinger, it's possible to judge how healthy and well muscled a bird is by the density of the padding. There should be barely any ridge of bone detectable.

Knurl – A leather knot or "button" made at the end of any strap is called a knurl.

Lanneret – "Lanneret" is the correct terminology for a male Lanner Falcon.

Leash – The leash is traditionally crafted of leather and is used to attach the bird either to the falconer's glove or to the perch. There are many form factors and materials currently being used in modern variations of the leash.

Luggaret - A "luggaret" is a male Luggar Falcon.

Lure - A lure is fake quarry designed to mimic actual prey using skins, feathers, and other items. By teaching the raptor to strike the lure, the desired hunting behavior is modeled and reinforced.

Mail – "Mail" is the term for a raptor's breast feathers.

Make In – "Make in" is the term for carefully approaching a raptor while the bird is still on the kill.

Malar Stripe – A falcon's malar strip is comprised of dark feathers that form a streak just below the eye. It is believed the darker coloration cuts down on glare and is an aid in hunting. The malar stripe may also be called the facial stripe or eye stripe.

Man – "Manning" is the process of acclimating a raptor to the presence of the handler. When a raptor is comfortable around people, the bird is said to be "well manned."

Mandible – A bird's mandible is comprised of the upper and lower jaw and the beak.

Mangalah – The mangalah is a cuff that is used in Middle Eastern falconry in place of the falconer's glove or gauntlet. It is also called a mankalah.

Mantle – A bird is said to "mantle" when it stretches out its wings to hide food. The same term is used to describe this action paired with stretching out the leg on the same side out of the body as well.

Mew – The mew or mews is the secure enclosure in which a bird is housed, also called the hawk house.

Microhawking – "Microhawking" is the practice of hunting with smaller raptors like Kestrels, Sharp-Shins, or Sparrowhawks. This variation of the sport is popular with falconers living in suburbs with little access to open spaces.

Molt – The annual shedding of feathers in raptors is referred to as the "molt," which typically begins in the spring or early summer and finishes in the autumn. If a molt is to be successful the bird must be in good health and receiving proper nutrition.

Musket – "Musket" is the term for a male Sparrowhawk.

Mute – Both the fecal matter passed by a raptor and the act of defecation itself is called "mute."

Nare – The nare is the nasal opening of a bird located in the featherless area of skin adjacent to the beak called the cere.

Nictitating Membrane – A bird's nictitating membrane may also be referred to as the haw or the third eyelid. It is a thin, white membrane that moves independently of the eyelid itself and serves to protect the eye.

Pannel – "Pannel" is a term used in the UK for the stomach region of a bird.

Passage – Passage birds are trapped before one year of age or the term can apply to any birds that are wild in origin.

Patagial – The term "patagial" refers to a bird's "arm pit" region.

Pendant Feathers – In the UK the term "pendant feathers" refers to those that are located behind the thighs of the bird.

Pitch – The term pitch is a reference to the height reached by a falcon when it rises. From the pitch position, the bird will go into the stoop or dive to strike at prey or a lure.

Plumage – A general reference to a bird's feathers.

Preen Gland – The preen gland is located at the base of the bird's tail. It produces oil that is vital to the health of both the feathers and the beak and that also provides waterproofing material for the plumage. The oil is spread throughout the feathers by the act of preening.

Primaries – The primary feathers or just "primaries" are the source of main forward thrust during flight. On the wing, these are the feathers located closest to the tip and farthest away from the center of the body. In the UK they are referred to as beam feathers, flight feathers or phalangeal feathers.

Principals – The principles are the longest two feathers on a raptor's wing.

Put Over – To "put over" is the process of the contents of the crop being moved to the stomach. In the UK it is referred to as endew. To "put away her crop" means the bird has completely emptied the crop into the stomach.

Pygostyle – The pygostyle is the tail bone, which supports both the tail muscles and feathers.

Quarry – Any game hunted by the falconer and bird in partnership is referred to as the "quarry." Examples are rabbit, pheasant, crow, quail or squirrel.

Rake Away – Rake away is the action of a raptor pulling out of a flight or, in particular, out of a stoop or dive.

Rangle – Rangle are the small, smooth stones that birds ingest as a means of cleaning out the crop. The term refers to both the stones themselves and the action of consuming them.

Rectrices – Rectrices are paired tail feathers. Typically there are 12 tail feathers total.

Remiges – When referred to together, the primary and the secondary feathers are called remiges.

Ring Perch - A ring perch is formed from a circle of metal with padding on top where the raptor stands.

Robin – A "robin" is a male Hobby Falcon.

Rouse – Rousing is the action of a hawk raising and shaking its feathers. This is an aspect of grooming as well as a sign of relaxation and contentment.

Rufter – "Rufter" is the UK term for a versatile hood that can fit a number of birds. It is not a precise or well-finished piece and is primarily used for trapping birds.

Sakeret – A "Sakeret" is a male Saker falcon.

Sarcel – The UK term used to identify the outermost primary feather is "sarcel."

Scale – Scales are used by falconers to ensure that their birds remain at the correct weight to hunt and for the maintenance of good health.

Screen Perch – Screen perches are vertical screened panels with a bar on top where the raptor stands.

Secondaries – The secondaries are the wing feathers located just inside the primary feathers and closer to the body. They form the largest surface area on the wing. In the UK these feathers are called "flags."

Sharp – A bird is said to be "sharp" if the padding on either side of the keel or breast bone is recessed allowing the bone to be felt. This means the bird is overly thin. "Sharp" may also be a reference to the bird's mindset, indicating her mental condition is superior to her physical state.

Slice – When some birds defecate the material is ejected with a degree of force rather than dropping straight down. This is called a "slice."

Slip – The "slip" refers to the setup of the quarry so that it is in a position to be caught so that the bird has a good opportunity to make a flight at the prey.

Snite – The term "snite" means to sneeze

St. Hubert – St. Hubert is the patron saint of falconry and falconers.

Stoop – The stoop is the deep, rocket fast dive executed by a bird (usually a falcon) with wings folded.
Strike – There are two common definitions for "strike." One is the action of the bird hitting the prey, the other is the act of loosening the braces of the hood and removing the hood from the bird's head.

Superciliary Line – The superciliary line are the feathers above the eye, which can be likened to an eye brow.

Supraorbital Ridge – The brow bone or supraorbital ridge sits just above the eye. This structure will be poorly developed in immature birds.

Swivel – The swivel is a small metal joint that is placed between the leash and the jesses to prevent tangling, especially while the bird is on the perch.

Tail Guard - Accipiter tail feathers are brittle and are sometimes protected with a tail guard to prevent unnecessary breakage.

Talons – Talons are the raptor's elongated, sharp toenails.

Tarsus – The tarsus is the leg between the foot and first joint. This is the area where the anklet is placed.

Telemetry – Telemetry systems use small transmitters attached to the bird that send signals to a receiver for purposes of locating the bird. This is an evolution from centuries old practice of using bells.

Throw Up – To "throw up" is to pull out of a stoop and to rise again at a steep pitch or angle of ascent on fixed wings without flapping. This action typically follows a missed strike or as a means of avoiding an accident.

Tidbit – Tidbits are small pieces of meat used to feed the birds. In the UK they are referred to as "bechins."

Tiercel (American spelling) or **Tercel** (British spelling) – A tiercel is a male raptor. Technically, however, the term applies in particular to a male Peregrine Falcon.

Tiring – A "tiring" is a tough piece of meat and bone intended to keep a bird occupied for a long period of time while also conditioning the beak and exercising the neck and back muscles. Examples of tirings include chicken or pigeon wing removed at the shoulder, a rabbit or duck head, or a rabbit foreleg with much of the meat removed.

Although the term "tiring" is now used universally, to be completely accurate it must refer to material from a mammal while "plumage" refers to that from another bird.

Tomial Tooth - The tomial tooth is the second hook on a raptor's beak. It fits into a notch in the lower beak in a specialized adaption for breaking the neck of prey.

Trachea – The trachea is a tube located behind the bird's tongue, which leads to the lungs.

Train – The 12 tail feathers are referred to collectively as the train, or in older language as the retrices.

Turk's Head Knot – A Turk's Head knot is used at the top of the falcon hood to create a handle so the piece can be safely manipulated well and to serve a decorative purpose. This may take the form of two knots tied with a bead, or the use of plumes or feathers. Leather hoods may also be intricately tooled or crafted with contrasting colors.

Varvel – A varvel is a flat ring made of silver or brass that can be used for multiple purposes. It may be put at the end of long jesses that have no slit to serve as a point of attachment for the leash or as a quick release mechanism while hunting.

Vent - The vent is the external surface of the cloaca.

Wait On – A bird of prey is said to "wait on" when it soars in circles or hangs above the falconer on the wind waiting for the quarry.

Wake – This is a method of manning a bird that exposes the creature to a running stream of experiences while keeping the bird awake for an extended period of time.

Warble – A bird of prey is said to warble when it stretches both wings up and back simultaneously.

Washed Meat – Washed meat has bean allowed to soak in cold water until most of the nutrients are pulled out. This allows the falconer to give the bird a large amount of the material without it receiving a great deal of fat and calories. It is analgous to "diet" food in humans.

Weather – To weather a bird is to put it outside for air and sunshine, usually in a weathering yard where it is protected from dogs, other raptors, and potential predators. This gives the bird the chance to bathe, spread its wings, and have a greater feeling of freedom. Weathering yards are typically placed so that the falconer can watch the bird at all times.

Wing Butts – The wing butts are the forward angled sections of the wing that can be compared to wrists in humans.

Wing Over – To "wing over" is to make a mid-flight change in direction by flipping over, often executed in response to a change in direction on the part of prey.

Yagi – A Yagi is a hand-held antenna receiver held by the falconer as part of a telemetry system for locating a bird of prey wearing a transmitter.

Yarak – Yarak is the state of complete and total focus on the hunt seen in Accipiters. It is an Eastern term that describes that point when a bird's training, weight, and mental focus all come into perfect sync in the field.

Chapter 8 – Frequently Asked Questions

As I have indicated, you may well spend 20 years or longer in this sport and continue to learn more about its history and the fine nuances of acquiring, training, and working with a raptor. For many enthusiasts, that very fact is a huge draw to become involved in falconry. The following, however, are some of the most common questions asked by people exploring the sport for the first time.

Can I legally own a bird of prey?

First, let me emphasize that all questions of legality must be addressed on a local, state, provincial, regional, and national level. Your first step in becoming a falconer is to find out what is legal for you in your location. (See Chapter 4 – Overview of Training Procedures for a lengthier explanation.)

To give you a short answer, in the United States, you may own a bird of prey provided you have a falconry license and are in possession of all the other required permits and licenses. In the United Kingdom, it is only legal to own a bird that has been bred and raised in captivity.

May I own more than one bird?

Again, this is a matter of legality that must be explored for your specific location. In the United States, however, while you are still an apprentice falconer, you are only allowed to have one bird, which is either a Red-Tailed Hawk or a Kestrel.

Do single birds do well living alone?

Birds of prey are naturally very solitary animals during all phases of their lives except the breeding season. Your captive raptor will be fine as an "only child," and although such a bird is certainly not a "pet," it will derive its own kind of satisfaction from its hunting and working relationship with you.

Do I need some kind of cage?

Raptors are not kept in cages like other birds, but are rather housed in sizable enclosures called mews. This area may be a separate structure, one that is attached to the house, or even a converted area within the house.

In the United States, apprentice falconers under the direction of a master falconer must build their mews in order to earn their falconry license. The structure must be inspected and approved by a game warden before the apprentice is allowed to acquire a bird.

I just release this bird and it comes back to me?

When you say it that way, you make the falcon sound like some kind of living boomerang, but yes, that's the theory. When you are out in the field, you release the bird and begin to flush game for the creature to hunt.

When you are done for the day or want to change location, you use a signal to call the bird down to the fist or glove. Most falconers do take the precaution of outfitting their birds with telemetry transmitters in case they have to go looking for the bird.

But, in the best of all scenarios, the falconer signals, and the raptor comes to the glove to be taken home. It certainly does happen that a bird will suddenly decide to fly away and resume its wild existence, but the deeper the bond forged between falconer and raptor, the less likely the chance that this will occur.

Are birds ever released to the wild?

Yes, some falconers will trap a bird in the fall, hunt with the raptor into the spring, and then release the bird back into the wild. Other falcons will keep a bird for many years before setting it free. Raptors that are returned to the wild, even those born in captivity that have imprinted on humans, do well when released and will breed with their wild cousins.

Why do raptors come back to the fist?

As part of the training, birds used in falconry are taught to return to the falconer to get food. Although they can clearly return to the wild when released for the hunt, the vast majority comes back to the fist reliably, even if they have only recently been trapped.

Remember, these are highly intelligent creatures that quickly come to associate the falconer with high quality food, a safe place to live, and protection. Birds intentionally released to the wild often come back to their mews, either the next day or even the next season. They clearly understand the relationship with the falconer as one that is highly advantageous to them.

When a wild animal is protected from the elements, kept in warm and dry conditions, and fed routinely, they interpret the situation accurately and act accordingly, even if that means being in relationship with man.

Are raptors starved into compliance?

Falconry does not involve starving the birds, but rather managing their weight just as a star athlete tracks their intake in relation to their muscle mass.

No athlete, including a raptor, can perform to peak potential without the right balance of weight and physical conditioning. Birds of prey should be weighed and exercised daily.

To be effective hunters, a raptor needs sufficient energy and reserves of fat to hunt for hours on end. A bird that is starved cannot possibly do that.

What do raptors eat?

Dietary guidelines vary by species and are meant to replicate the bird's wild diet. Typically the captive diet will consists of some combination of rodents, quail, pigeon, chicken, rabbit, insects, and beef.

Falconers work to get the best balance of nutrients possible from these food sources, which are also routinely supplemented by soaking in vitamin and mineral formulas.

Do falconers raise food for their birds?

Raising food for your bird of prey is an option, but one that is purely a matter of personal preference. You can raise pigeons, chickens, quail, or rabbits as food animals, but many people find that process emotionally difficult or overly expensive and labor intensive.

Another option is simply to store the prey the raptor catches to be used as food, supplementing with thawed frozen meats that have been purchased. Again, this is a matter of personal preference.

Does the bird bring the catch back?

No, it is not normal for a raptor to just drop the catch at your feet. Their training teaches them to follow the falconer and strike on game that has been flushed. If, for instance, that is a rabbit, even a very large Red-Tailed Hawk would have difficulty bringing the carcass to the hunter.

When the bird has done its job, it is then your turn to do yours, locating the bird and its quarry. It is possible that the prey will still be alive. In this case, you must dispatch the struggling animal in a quick and humane fashion.

Can I take a raptor out in public?

It would be a mistake to start thinking of your raptor as a

pet on a leash. Certainly some birds do perfectly well in public and are used for purposes of education and demonstration at schools or similar venues. It's quite common to see birds of prey being flown at Renaissance Faires, for instance.

It is not common, however, for a falconer to just take the bird on errands. Typically the birds are not removed from their mews for any purpose other than hunting, and in some areas, it may not be legal to have a bird of prey in a public setting.

Again, on all matters pertaining to legality, verify the exact details for your location and then use your best judgment with the welfare of the bird front and center in your decision-making process.

Can you hunt any time?

As far as the bird is concerned, yes, but state, provincial, and national laws determine what game may be taken, in what manner, and during what time period.

The bird must also go through an annual moult, when they lose their feathers and grow a new set. Since this takes a tremendous amount of energy, the birds are not used for hunting during this time, but rather stay in the mews and weathering yard.

Typically birds are allowed to molt over the summer months, with hunting activities resuming in the fall. It is imperative that raptors be well fed during molting to ensure that the process is successful and that the new feathers are healthy.

What is the lifespan of the birds?

Lifespan will vary widely by species, but raptors stand a far better chance of living into a productive old age in captivity than in the wild. Some Harris Hawks have lived 25 years in captivity, while 12 is positively ancient in the wild.

Estimates suggest that 70% of the birds of prey that hatch in the wild will die before reaching one year of age, with 90% of the survivors never making five years. They succumb to starvation, wounds from larger predators, parasites, freezing, and often vehicular collisions.

Certainly raptors used for hunting face their own slate of dangers, but they are also well fed, sheltered from the elements and predators, and benefit from veterinary care. Many such birds continue to hunt actively into their 20s.

Are my other pets in any danger?

Yes. Be extremely cautious with cats and small dogs, which the birds easily mistake for prey animals. Clearly any kind of pet rodent or rabbit is in extreme danger.

The only way to safely have other pets and a raptor is to maintain excellent security around the mews and weathering yard, to maintain control of the bird at all times, and to prevent any interactions.

Do raptors attack on command?

There are no commands issued to signal a raptor to attack an intended prey animal. Hunting is an instinct for these birds. They need only a visual cue – simply seeing the intended quarry -- to begin to hunt.

What is the purpose of the hood?

The hood is a highly familiar element of the sport that most people readily associate with falconry. It has been used for centuries, and is a tool to control the visual nature of the birds.

By limiting what the hawk sees, the falconer also controls its reactions and keeps the bird calm. If falcons cannot see something that would frighten them, they don't get scared. It's just that simple.

Clearly the bird has to be accustomed to the sights it will routinely encounter when the hood is not in place, but for those times when the raptor is taken into settings where it could easily become upset, the hood is an indispensible calming tool.

What is the time commitment?

Initially, you must spend several hours a day working with the bird over a period of several weeks or even months. As soon as the bird masters the basics, it can be taken out hunting. This may need to be a daily activity for young birds or for given species.

Over time, as the bird's level of experience grows and the bond with the falconer deepens, outings may occur a few times a week or a month, but this does not lessen the need for interaction on days when the bird remains in the mews.

Raptors should be weighed daily, checked for overall well-being, and fed. The mews, perches, bath pan, and weathering yard all should be kept clean. These routine chores may take less than an hour, but they are still an important part of "manning" the bird to keep it tame.

Since there may be no one to whom you can pass on these responsibilities, you must weigh your other commitments against your desire to become a falconer. Do your work, travel, and family schedules allow you to take on being a falconer? Do you have an area or have access to an area where you can hunt?

Review the material in Chapter 4 – Overview of Training Procedures for more information, and consider joining a local falconry group, even if you do not yet have a bird, to begin to get a feel for living this lifestyle.

Remember that if this is not the right time in your life for you to own and hunt with a bird, you can still be an active supporter of falconry as a sport and participate as an advocate and spectator.

What is the hardest part of the sport?

It's very difficult to give a definitive answer to a question like, "What's the hardest part of the sport?" There are certainly financial considerations to mull over, and the problem all suburban falconers face of just finding a place to hunt. Clashing and overlapping commitments to work and family plague other people.

But I think it is also important to emphasize that we are discussing a blood sport. Unless you are flying a very small bird like a Kestrel that may just happily go after grasshoppers and the like, other animals will die. If the raptor doesn't kil the quarry, you have to. Are you up for that? Can you quickly and humanely put an animal out of its suffering?

Matters of logistics can be worked out and overcome, but you either have the mental discipline to hunt in this very elemental way or you do not. That is a point about which you must be brutally honest with yourself.

Is there field etiquette?

If you are invited to go hunting with a falconer, there are no rules or rituals of hawking similar to those you might see in an elaborate foxhunt, but there are some things you need to know.

First, you should absolutely never touch another falconer's bird without express permission. You may unsettle the bird, and you can easily get bitten. Also, do not wear any item trimmed in fur, which a raptor can mistake for prey. Keep yourself warm with some other material!

Be respectful and let the falconer guide any and all

interactions you do or do not have with the bird. Follow the falconer's lead at all times.

In the field, walk on the opposite side from that on which the falconer is holding the bird, which will typically be to the right. Understand that birds of prey don't like strangers to be too close to them, or behind them. Keep up and keep to the right.

Don't make sudden movements or loud noises near the bird unless directed to do so by the falconer in the interest of flushing quarry.

When the bird takes a game animal, stay behind the falconer as he retrieves the quarry. Do not attempt to help. If the falconer hands you quarry or a lure, keep these items out of the bird's sight.

Remember that you are there to learn. Watch what the falconer is doing. How does he handle the bird? The equipment? How does he interact with the bird? With dogs if they are present? How does he take quarry from the bird? Or dispatch wounded quarry if necessary?

The middle of a hunt is likely not the best time to ask questions, but make mental notes of the things you want to ask later. Most falconers are quite happy to discuss their sport and their bird – usually at length.

How do I get started?

In Chapter 4 – Overview of Training, I discuss the steps

necessary to become a falconer in the United States and review the basics of training. The legal procedures will vary by state and province, but the main principles of training are fairly universal. But remember, you have a lot to learn before you even think about getting your own bird!

I highly recommend that you locate and join the nearest local falconry group. You will also want to locate and join online discussion communities. Don't just go blundering in to either group setting! You are new to the culture of falconry. Listen much more than you talk and take notes on what you are learning.

Attend falconry meets or exhibitions, and, if possible, go on a hunt or hunts with a master falconer. If you remain firm in your commitment to join the sport, take the next step by contacting the correct governing authority. In the United States, that will be your state's Department of Fish and Wildlife.

You will receive a packet of information that will outline the necessary steps to take to earn your falconry license. (Again, legal requirements and procedures vary by location.)

Afterword

Falconry is, oddly enough, both a straightforward, simple sport, and a deeply complex one. The methods used to catch a raptor, and then to train the bird as a hunting companion are not difficult. Anyone can master the techniques. Only time and patience are required.

But the bond that develops between the falconer and his bird is a harder thing to quantify. One of the most difficult things to accept is that after hours of training a bird, the hawk always has the option of simply flying away and returning to its former life.

When a raptor does not do that, but chooses instead to alight on the glove, the feeling for the falconer is somewhat humbling. The bird is making a choice, placing a responsibility on your shoulders that you must continue to meet.

Birds of prey are not pets, and yet falconers have deep affection for the birds they fly. The loss of a bird is no small matter to someone genuinely dedicated to the animal's care and welfare.

I hope that I have been able to provide you with a comprehensive introduction to the ancient sport of falconry. My goal was to help you appreciate the richness and length of the tradition and to come to understand the types of birds that are flown.

In describing the training process, I've tried to strike the middle ground of methodology, while acknowledging that all master falconers have their own "formulas" for preparing to enter a bird on a given quarry.

It should also be noted that methods vary by species, and I have opted to take a "beginner's bird" approach to this text. Very few falconers ever fly a single bird, or stay with the same species throughout their career. Once you have flown a raptor, the desire to fly other birds can be overwhelming.

Falconry truly is a lifestyle, a sport in which you will make life-long friends, and in whose unique sub-culture you will become quickly immersed. When a room full of falconers is talking "shop," outsiders are often hard pressed to know if they're still speaking English!

It is for this reason that I opted to eschew a traditional glossary in favor of a complete chapter on terminology, some of which does not appear in my text at all. In the apprentice stage of your career, you will find yourself looking up terms constantly just to keep up with what's being said!

I remember with no small humor the very frustrated apprentice who exclaimed, "My God! There's a name for the little leather things you tie the bells on with?" Yes, there is. They're called bewits.

Admittedly, there's a great deal arcane about this sport, but then there is also much of modernity. For more than 15 years, falcons patrolled the runways at JFK in New York driving away nuisance birds so planes could take off and land safely at the busy airport.

If you decide that you have the time, mental discipline, and discretionary funds to commit to studying falconry and perfecting your skills as a falconer in the coming years, your life will be greatly enhanced by your association with these stunning raptors.

You may never completely understand the mind of your bird, but a kind of communication will develop between you. That partnership, the place where the hunting instincts of two diverse species intersect, is for falconers the great unquantifiable joy of this sport.

Appendix I – State / Provincial Wildlife Agencies

Alabama Game & Fish Division
http://www.dcnr.state.al.us/agfd

Alaska Fish and Game Department
http://www.state.ak.us/local/akpages/FISH.GAME/adfghome.htm

Arizona Game and Fish Department
http://www.azgfd.gov

Arkansas Game and Fish Commission
http://www.agfc.state.ar.us

California Department of Fish and Game
http://www.dfg.ca.gov

Colorado Department of Natural Resources
http://www.dnr.state.co.us/

Connecticut Department of Environmental Protection
http://www.dep.state.ct.us

Delaware Department of Natural Resources and Environmental Controls
http://www.dnrec.state.de.us/

Florida Fish and Wildlife Conservation Commission
http://www.floridaconservation.org/

Georgia Department of Natural Resources

http://www.dnr.state.ga.us/
Hawaii Department of Land and Natural Resources
http://www.hawaii.gov/dlnr/

Idaho Department of Fish and Game
http://www.state.id.us/fishgame/fishgame.html

Illinois Department of Natural Resources
dnr.state.il.us

Indiana Department of Natural Resources
http://www.in.gov/dnr

Iowa Department of Natural Resources
http://www.iowadnr.com/

Kansas Dept. of Wildlife and Parks
http://www.ink.org/public/kdwp/

Kentucky Department of Fish and Wildlife Resources
http://www.state.ky.us/agencies/fw/kdfwr.htm

Louisiana Department of Wildlife and Fisheries
http://www.wlf.state.la.us

Maine Department of Conservation
http://www.maine.gov/doc/

Maine Inland Fisheries and Wildlife
http://www.maine.gov/ifw/

Maryland Department of Natural Resources

http://www.dnr.state.md.us/index.asp

Massachusetts Department of Fish and Game
http://www.mass.gov/dfwele/

Michigan Department of Natural Resources
http://www.michigan.gov/dnr

Minnesota Department of Natural Resources
http://www.dnr.state.mn.us/

Mississippi Department of Wildlife, Fisheries and Parks
http://www.mdwfp.com

Missouri Department of Conservation
mdc.mo.gov/

Montana Fish, Wildlife & Parks
http://www.fwp.mt.gov

Montana Natural Resource Information Center
nris.state.mt.us/

Nebraska Game and Parks Commission
outdoornebraska.ne.gov

Nevada Department of Wildlife
http://www.ndow.org

New Hampshire Fish and Game Department
http://www.wildlife.state.nh.us

New Jersey Dept. of Fish and Wildlife

http://www.state.nj.us/dep/fgw

New Mexico Department of Game and Fish
http://www.wildlife.state.nm.us/

New York Department of Environmental Conservation
http://www.dec.ny.gov/

North Carolina Wildlife Resources Commission
http://www.ncwildlife.org/index.htm

North Dakota Game and Fish Department
gf.nd.gov/

Ohio Department of Natural Resources
http://www.dnr.state.oh.us/wildlife/default.htm

Oklahoma Department of Wildlife Conservation
http://www.state.ok.us/~odwc/

Oregon Fish and Wildlife Service
http://www.dfw.state.or.us

Pennsylvania Department of Conservation and Natural
Resources
http://www.dcnr.state.pa.us

Pennsylvania Fish and Boat Commission
http://www.fish.state.pa.us/mpag1.htm

Pennsylvania Game Commission
http://www.pgc.state.pa.us/

Rhode Island Department of Environmental Management
http://www.dem.ri.gov

South Carolina Department of Natural Resources
http://www.dnr.state.sc.us/

South Dakota Department of Game, Fish and Parks
http://www.sdgfp.info/

Tennessee Wildlife Resources Agency
http://www.state.tn.us/twra/

Texas Parks and Wildlife Department
http://www.tpwd.state.tx.us/

Utah Division of Wildlife Resources
wildlife.utah.gov/dwr/

Vermont Department of Fish and Wildlife
http://www.anr.state.vt.us/fw/fwhome/

Virginia Department of Conservation & Recreation
http://www.dcr.virginia.gov/

Virginia Department of Game and Inland Fisheries
http://www.dgif.state.va.us/

Washington Department of Fish and Wildlife
wdfw.wa.gov/

West Virginia Natural Heritage Program

http://www.wvdnr.gov/wildlife/wdpintro.shtm
West Virginia Division of Natural Resources
http://www.wvdnr.gov/

Wisconsin Dept. of Natural Resources
http://www.dnr.state.wi.us

Wyoming Department of Game and Fish
gf.state.wy.us

Canada

Alberta Sustainable Resource Development (SRD)
http://www.srd.gov.ab.ca/fishwildlife

Manitoba Wildlife
http://www.gov.mb.ca/conservation/wildlife

Ontario Ministry of Natural Resources
http://www.mnr.gov.on.ca/en/Business/FW

Quebec Natural Resources
http://www.mrnf.gouv.qc.ca/english/home.jsp

Canadian Wildlife Service (Environment Canada)
http://www.ec.gc.ca/default.asp?lang=En&n=FD9B0E51-1

Source: North American Falconers Association, http://www.n-a-f-a.com, accessed August 2014.

Relevant Websites

Cetrero.com (Spain)
http://www.cetrero.com/portal.htm

Welsh Hawking Club
http://www.eclipse.co.uk/admiralc

Arkansas Hawking Association
falconrynarkansas.org

Arab Falconers
clubs.yahoo.com/clubs/arabfalconers

Arizona Falconers' Assoicaiton
http://www.ctaz.com/~ladyhawk/AFA.html

Arizona Hawking Club
azfalconry.com

Associazione Falconeria Marchigiana (Italy)
digilander.iol.it/artevenandicumavibus

Association Québécoise des Fauconniers et Autoursiers
(Canada)
http://www.geocities.com/Yosemite/Rapids/5343/

Aztec Falconry
http://www.hail.icestorm.net/ddavalos/default.html

British Columbia Falconry Association
http://www.dreamwater.com/falconrybc

British Falconcers' Club
http://www.britishfalconersclub.co.uk

British Hawking Association
http://www.bhassoc.org/index1.htm

Central Falconry and Raptor Club
http://www.central-falconry.co.uk

Cheshire Hawking Club
http://www.cheshirehawkingclub.co.uk

Czech Falconers Club (Czechoslovakia)
http://www.sokolnictvi.net

Dartmoor Hawking School of Falconry
http://www.dartmoorhawking.co.uk

Falconers De Les Comarques de Barcelona (Spain)
http://www.falconersdelescomarquesdebarcelona.com/fcb/

Falkirk Falconry in the Blair Drummond Safari Park, Scotland
http://www.falkirkfalconry.com

Florida Hawking Fraternity
http://www.f-h-f.org

Georgia Falconry Association
http://www.georgiafalconryassociation.com

Hawk Board
http://www.hawkboard-cff.org.uk

Hungarian Falconers Club
solymaszat.uw.hu

International Association for Falconry and Conservation of Birds of Prey
http://www.i-a-f.org

Ireland's School of Falconry
http://www.falconry.ie

International Falconer Magazine
http://www.intfalconer.net

Irish Hawking Club
http://www.irishhawkingclub.ie

Independent Bird Register
http://www.ibr.org.uk

Maryland Falconers Association
http://www.marylandfalconry.com

New Jersey Falconry Club
geocities.com/jerseyfalconryclub

Nevada Falconry Apprentice Program
home.earthlink.net/~cfalconer

North Carolina Falconer's Guild
http://www.ncfalconersguild.org

Northamptonshire Raptor Club
http://www.northamptonshireraptorclub.co.uk

Ohio Falconry Association
http://www.ohiofalconry.org

Oregon Falconers Association
http://www.oregonfalconers.org/index.html
Oregon Falconers Association

Russian Falconry Association
http://www.aolp.ru

Scottish Hawking Club
http://www.scottishhawkingclub.co.uk

Southeastern Raptor Rehabilitation Center
http://www.vetmed.auburn.edu/raptor

Southwestern Falconers Association
http://www.geocities.com/Yosemite/Rapids/3304

Ssociazione Italiana per la Falconeria (Italy)
http://www.falconeriaitaliana.com

Schweizerische Falknervereinigung (Switzerland)
http://www.falknerei.ch

Svenska Falkenerarförbundet (Swedish Falconry Association)
storm.f2o.org

Texas Hawking Association
http://www.geocities.com/texashawking/tha.html

The Hawking Center
http://www.thehawkingcentre.co.uk

The North American Falconers Association
http://www.n-a-f-a.org

Virginia Falconers Association
vafalconry.swva.net

Washington Falconers Associaton
http://www.wafalconry.org

Wingspan Birds of Prey Trust
http://www.wingspan.co.nz

Wyoming Falconers' Association
http://www.wyomingfalconers.org

Conclusion

Thank you again for buying this book! I spent months writing it. As someone who has loved falconry for years, friends told me to share my knowledge!

I hope this book helped you decide if you wish to take up this wonderful pastime. If you do I hope you have many happy years enjoying everything it has to offer.

Please Help....

Finally, if you enjoyed this book, please, please, please take the time to share your thoughts and post a review on whatever site you purchased it from. It will be greatly appreciated!

Don't Forget

I've got a great collection of falconry videos that I'd like to share with you totally free.

Please just visit

http://www.FalconryGift.com – For your free videos

Index

FREE Falconry Videos – Don't Forget...

Before I go any further I want to share with a fabulous collection of falconry videos

Please just visit

http://www.FalconryGift.com so we can email all the videos 100% free – just as an extra 'thank you' for purchasing this book.

The videos cover things like

-   Introduction
-   Getting Started
-   Telemetry
-   Training
-   Hoods
-   Lure
-   And lots more

Make sure you receive them free at

http://www.FalconryGift.com (it's free)

CPSIA information can be obtained
at www.ICGtesting.com
Printed in the USA
FSHW021251161218
54516FS